STEP INTO
YOUR
BRILLIANT
PURPOSE

COMPILED BY
REBECCA HALL GRUYTER & MAUREEN RYAN BLAKE
#1 INTERNATIONAL BEST SELLING AUTHORS

Step Into Your Brilliant Purpose

Copyright © 2022 by Rebecca Hall Gruyte

RHG Media Productions

25495 Southwick Drive #103

Hayward, CA 94544

All rights reserved. No part of this publication may be reproduced distributed or transmitted in any form or by any means including photocopying recording or other electronic or mechanical means without proper written permission of author or publisher, except in the case of brief quotations embodied in critical reviews and certain other noncommercial uses permitted by copyright law.

IISBN 978-1-7374041-2-5 (paperback)

Visit us on line at www.YourPurposeDrivenPractice.com

Printed in the United States of America.

CONTENTS

Preface ..... Rebecca Hall Gruyter, Compiler
and Maureen Ryan Blake, Compiler 7

Section 1: Connect with Your Purpose

Making a Difference, One Story at a Time	By Maureen Famiano 11
Find Your Muhammad Ali Strength	By Abbey Daw 19
Stepping into Your Soul's Purpose	By Sam Yau 27
Grief: A Catalyst and Opportunity for Positive Change	By Janet Schmidt 35
Choose to Fully Live	By S. Dawn Bradford 43

Section 2: Step into Your Brilliant Purpose

Shine in Your Purpose!	By Maureen Ryan Blake 53
Lean Into the Invisible to be Visible	By Hilary DeCesare 63
Brilliant Success for Rebels	By Charlotte Allen 71
The Courage to Face Your Purpose	By Kara Goss 79
Rituals	By Nitya Garg, Naveli Garg, and Manisha Gupta 87

Section 3: Step Forward and Shine!

Shine in Your Brilliance!	By Rebecca Hall Gruyter 97
Let Forgiveness Color Your World	By MacKenzie Nelson 105
The Decided Heart Effect	By Sonja Montiel and Hilary Bilbrey 111
Declutter to Step Into Your Purpose	By Alison Kero 119

Closing Thoughts ..... Rebecca Hall Gruyter, Compiler
and Maureen Ryan Blake, Compiler 127

ACKNOWLEDGEMENTS

When writing an anthology, it takes many voices willing to join together to bring forth the book in a powerful and united way. It has been such an honor and privilege to work with this amazing group of experts and influencers. We want to thank these amazing leaders for entrusting us to bring forth and share their powerful stories.

Thank you to our amazing teams, communities, families, and friends for leaning in, cheering us on, and saying yes to help us bring this book forward so powerfully. It takes many hearts and spirits coming together, bringing their gifts and talents to the mix to bring something like this book forward in multiple formats. We couldn't do it without all of you, and thank you for leaning in and helping us all share out this transformational information so beautifully.

PREFACE

Rebecca Hall Gruyter, Compiler and Maureen Ryan Blake, Compiler

Thank you for leaning into this powerful anthology! We are honored and excited to bring this powerful book featuring seventeen experts that are committed to helping you step into your brilliant purpose. We want to support you in tapping into the wisdom we have discovered and believe will empower and support you on your journey.

Our vision is to have our experts share insights, tips, and tools we have discovered to support and empower you on your journey. We know that life is not a solo journey, and by coming together, our goal is to help you step further into and more powerfully into your gifts, talents, and abilities. Together, as we lift each other up, we are all able to grow, reach more people, and have a greater impact than we do trying to do everything on our own.

In each chapter, our authors will equip and empower you to step forward more fully. We believe this book is a living and interactive book that will speak wisdom, encouragement, and power into your life. We want to invite you to pause, take a deep breath, and be ready to receive these powerful chapters so they can ignite a fire in you, inspire courage in you, and focus you on stepping fully into bringing forward the gift of who you are and all that you are called to be.

Here is how to get the most out of this powerful book. The book is divided into three sections; each one is designed to meet you exactly where you are and to support you in each step of your journey. **In the first section, Connect to Your Purpose,** we help you connect more fully with you, your truth, and your purpose. **In the second section, Step into Your Brilliant Purpose,** our experts share how to step into your gifts and talents and choose to live in a positive and empowered way. **In the third section, Step Forward and SHINE!,**

our experts share with you how to move forward with your purpose and shine your gifts out into the world. At the end of each powerful chapter, you will find the author's biography and contact information. We encourage you to "friend" and follow those authors with whom you feel a powerful resonance and connection so that they can continue to pour into you and support you on your journey in life.

Now the next step is yours. Drink in the insights, tips, and wisdom that are within these pages to serve, support, and inspire you. Take the time to pause, read, and reflect. Listen to the powerful messages of hope that are waiting for you within the pages of this book. It's not an accident that you purchased this book and are opening it to read. We invite you to lean in and truly receive the messages and wisdom that will speak to your heart and soul that you will find in these transformational and dynamic pages. Enjoy this rich collection of wisdom, insight, and encouragement being provided by our amazing authors. We can't wait to see you stepping into and shining in your brilliant purpose!

Rebecca Hall Gruyter and Maureen Ryan Blake, Book Compilers

Rebecca Hall Gruyter is the founder/owner of Your Purpose Driven Practice and CEO of RHG Media Productions.

Maureen Ryan Blake is the founder of the Power of the Tribe Network.

SECTION 1:

Connect with Your Purpose

MAKING A DIFFERENCE, ONE STORY AT A TIME
BY MAUREEN FAMIANO

Lights. Camera. Action. Being a television producer was a cool job. I met a lot of interesting people, saw fun behind-the-scenes events, and loved creating engaging shows for our audience. I was living my best life. Booking guests on a television morning show was really fun. Every day was different. As the executive producer of the syndicated talk show *Daytime in Tampa Bay*, I worked to find unique stories and great guest opportunities. After years in news, I moved into programming to showcase the amazing positive stories. I felt they were missing, and I looked for a platform to share them. I'd search for *the* best story to show people there *is* good news. There are stories and people that put kindness first. It's the news I felt people needed and wanted to hear. I searched for it and always found it.

I remember one pretty epic day at our NBC studio. I had booked music mogul David Foster on the show. It was a huge deal after dozens of emails to make it happen. A grand piano was delivered to the TV station. A superstar set was created. The hosts and crew were super excited to have this amazing talent coming to our show. Foster worked with Celine Dion, Whitney Houston, and many more, creating so many popular hits. All the hard work leading up to his arrival was worth it. He was very impressed with our studio and team. He even agreed to play some jingles after the interview segment and musical performance wrapped up. He was truly over-the-top incredible, down to earth, and just awesome to work with; he couldn't have been nicer. His visit was memorable, but there was something nagging at me. It was a mystery, and when I least remembered, it would pop back in my head. The "it" was something I noticed weeks before. Something was happening. I didn't know what. I tried to forget and immerse myself in all things work and family, but when I stopped, the worry cropped up. What was it? I didn't know. The fantastic work success was overshadowed by the unknown. It was a sobering reminder I had to find out what was wrong. I hoped it was nothing and wanted to cross it off my list and get on to more work and family needs.

It all began in the summer of 2010. I noticed signs and thought, *what's that?* I delayed a doctor's visit and hoped it would go away. It did not. It was there when I went to the bathroom. Even as I changed my diet, the blood in my stool remained. A visit to my primary led to a specialist referral and then, after a few weeks, a colonoscopy to determine the issue. It turned out there was a *big* problem. A small, kiwi-size tumor was discovered. It had to be tested and biopsied. My battle began.

The cloud of uncertainty was thick. I will never forget the words, "*You have cancer. Colon cancer.*" It echoed in my mind. What? Who, me? By then, I suspected something was wrong, and that was the case. Now I had to go into a fight mode. I had to determine my next best steps. I learned it's the third leading cancer-causing death in the US. It was ironic to me I was dealing with the biggest breaking news story of my life. I attacked it like my work. I had to really go into production mode. I had to produce the best show of my life. The show of me fighting and winning this unexpected event. I had to be here for my kids and family. I had to live.

In a whirlwind of scheduling, I searched and set up appointments and met with three surgeons to get my prognosis and opinions. I wanted options. I ended up opting for surgery first instead of going a chemotherapy route, as some had suggested. It was a last-minute decision, but I believed in the surgeon, one of the best in Tampa Bay. The surgery went fine. Then healing. My abdomen had seen better days, but I got through it. I thought I was done. Weeks later, my checkup proved I wasn't done. The tumor had penetrated the lymph nodes. This confirmed a stage-three colon cancer diagnosis and a new fight. I chose an aggressive one-two punch with a combination of chemotherapy and radiation. That battle lasted one full year.

It began with six rounds of chemo then breaks to get stronger. Then twenty-eight days of radiation. Then a break, followed by four more rounds of chemo. It was grueling at times. Throughout it all, the support of family and friends was awesome. Meal trains fed my family, and prayers gave me much strength. It was an odd time for me as I was always the energizer bunny. I would run circles around people who would ask how I was involved in so many things. I would laugh it off and say, "I don't know; I just do it." Now though, I was in pause mode, reflective, quiet. The running had stopped. I had to pause and fight.

Once complete, follow-ups meant colonoscopies each year. No problem. I was good to go. I beat cancer! I won. I am grateful and blessed. Onward.

Back to full-on work with projects and exciting new television show guests and opportunities. Community projects that I sunk my teeth into. Kids' events, including baseball and softball. I was getting stronger. I could do things with my family again after saying, "No, you go" for a year. I now had a new notch on my belt and attacked every day with my can-do attitude to live each day to the fullest. I was a survivor.

All was fine for six years, and then, *it was not fine.* A whopping twenty polyps were discovered in a routine colonoscopy. Polyps can become cancerous. They needed to go. At that time, a surgeon said he could take time to remove them, and that was that. Great. The very next year, twenty-two new polyps were discovered in another routine colonoscopy. I was in shock. *Again? What?* It was a gut punch. I got opinions from three surgeons who all said the same thing. I would need my colon removed, which meant having a bag or ileostomy for the rest of my life. What? No. I couldn't live with that.

I was at wit's end and believed there must be another option. It was a soul-searching few weeks of surgeon meetings and assessments, the medical weight bearing down on me while I juggled a busy career and family needs. Finally, a medical friend suggested another surgeon who gave me hope without a bag. It was the hope and the answer I was searching for. That fourth opinion was really a life-changing meeting. While it did mean a six-month journey with a temporary ileostomy (bag), I trusted in the final hoped-for outcome. The whopping eight-hour surgery to remove my colon was daunting and epic. After getting the temporary ileostomy, it meant a journey with wound care, and learning how to eat and digest food was unbelievably challenging. I had to figure out what to eat, meal by meal. Some things worked; other food did not. It was challenging, frustrating, painful at times, and defeating.

When the time was right, the ileostomy reversal surgery took place. The newly created pouch worked. My body had to adapt again. It's been a long journey to this very day. I am so glad I didn't accept my original fate. My tenacity for asking lots of questions all the time led me to options that gave me my life now, complete with adventure, productivity, and accomplishment. A never-give-up spirit and positivity powered me through.

It's been four years since the reversal. I have my life back and am so grateful. I often reflect on the meeting of that fourth surgeon and the game-changer it was for me. If I hadn't sought options, I would have settled for what I was being told. I did not settle. I never do.

It's ironic; my stage-three colon cancer diagnosis was the same that *Black Panther* star Chadwick Boseman faced. His heroic, quiet battle stunned the world when his death was announced in September 2020. The news hit me hard. **We battled the same disease. He sadly lost his battle, yet I am still here. It still gives me pause. I believe there is more I am supposed to do.**

Work and family life took on new meaning again. I often said through the journey the Lord was saying, "Okay, if you don't slow down and are go, go, go, I'll stop you. Take this." I managed and beat colon cancer. I was back to busy, busy and juggle, juggle, and he said, "You didn't listen, so take this round two." So I forged through that too. It was quite something, both of those journeys. **The lessons I learned were not to give up. To encourage others to get tested, encourage others to go to the doctor, and the importance of connecting with others. I was a living, breathing example of that positive get-'er-done mentality to win. Perhaps that was the bigger goal all along. My surgeon called me Super Woman. I laughed and thought,** *Nope, just determined.*

My family has always been very important to me—I'm their biggest cheerleader. My son and daughter are wonderful kids. My husband is pretty terrific too. I remind them life is a gift; find your passion and believe. I guide and encourage. I am no-nonsense, and sometimes that's not appreciated, but they know I speak from the heart. Life is hard, but you can power through. I try to help them navigate life's curves. During my health challenges, I remained strong and determined, perhaps too strong for my family to really understand what I was going through. I made it look easy. They saw me do it, and only now do my kids as young adults realize what I went through. It's funny, sharing my journey with a health care worker familiar with such a journey stopped in her tracks, hearing what I went through. I was surprised by her reaction because I just did it, and my family didn't really know or understand the gravity of all the challenges and the determined decisions I made because I was very strong. Her reaction validated my accomplishment.

This journey and the realization that I am still here to make a positive difference and do more led me to start my own business, MEFMedia, right before the pandemic. I use my life lessons to help others; this is my purpose. **Everyone has a story, but many don't share it. They don't know how to. I do. Sharing may help others be stronger, power through, and understand they are not alone. This has become my purpose.** I enjoy people, and I listen well, and because of that, they tend to open up to me. They often tell me, "*I've never told anyone that*" or "*I haven't shared that with someone in decades.*" That's where the nuggets of loveliness are discovered; from there, we launch and grow. I help businesses and individuals strategize and shine the spotlight on their journeys. Having personally booked close to fifteen thousand TV guest interviews, I know when I hear the hook that makes them unique and the story that will make people listen up.

Client wins are proof I'm on the right path. One of our projects involved a wonderful principal giving back by creating a food pantry at school for her students during the pandemic. She had never done anything like that. I got her media attention, and Ellen DeGeneres show producers took note, and Ellen did a shoutout on her show and sent her financial contribution.

There was also a kidney transplant story that touched my heart. I offered media outreach to bring the story exposure. I didn't know the kidney recipient or donor very well, but I felt the story could change lives and give people hope during the pandemic. Now the transplant's complete, and both are doing great. The media attention helped more understand the transplant journey to consider donating too.

Finally, there's the story of a nonprofit giving blankets to the homeless. I got fantastic media exposure to showcase the huge need for this kindness mission. It really struck a chord locally, and drumroll . . . Lady Gaga's team even reached out in the midst of their Global Kindness initiative to recognize the blanket mission.

These are wins I'm proud of. These stories make a difference, and it brings me great joy to know that getting them into the media spotlight helps spread awareness and kindness. It's important to me.

My motto, "Together we win," is something I embrace and try to live out every day.

I'm a big believer in creating a community. Meeting people and making them feel they matter is important. I try to raise people up. My business gives me the ability to help others who don't know how to gain traction. I remind people to be genuine and authentic. Be passionate. If you really connect with people, it can be powerful. Sometimes, I feel the urge to share a thought or video of the day on social media. Often, it leads people to message me for advice or comfort as they go through life's challenges. My post leads to reactions and rich conversations. That reaffirms I am here to share those thoughts to help others know they are not alone and offer hope. We can each choose to lift others up, to share our journey, and look for those positive messages/nuggets to share out.

When it comes to business and strategy, I remind people to think about what makes them unique and different. How are they relatable? When they meet people, what do *they* look for, and how do they connect? Having important conversations is enriching. Look for things that set others apart and share your uniqueness too. That's how people will remember you. It's how you connect that leads to a bond.

We all remember those discoveries in conversations that are true treasures that lead to "that happened to me" moments or "I went to that school" or "I'm a military brat too." Whatever it is, find that connection. I take that unusual or unique aspect of a business to make it a moment to treasure and brand. The media is always looking for angles. I was, so I know. People often bury their own best lead. I find that lead and use it to put them in the spotlight, making them stand out.

If I had to pick my superpower, it would be my positivity and kindness. No shield, just the power of being upbeat. I always find that silver lining. I think outside the box. *What box?* I have a creative side that makes me unstoppable in life and my career. I help people elevate their business or passion to the next level with new opportunities and community awareness. It's part of why, I believe, I'm still here. My tenacity led me to live to ask lots of questions and inspire others. Because I'm still here, I can help others be the best version of themselves too.

As I look to the future, I feel grateful and blessed. I will keep sharing the positive stories as I firmly believe we all win when kindness takes the lead. I

choose to make every day count—really count. At the end of the day, I know I've done all I could do. I do hope when people look back on me that it would give me great pride for people to say, "She's the one who got through some really tough times, but she did it with a smile, and she shared the stories about people that lifted us all up and made us all better."

Tips for Sharing Your Story:

1. What is your message? Your unique story and brand?
2. How can it connect with others?
3. Choose to get support and strategy in sharing your story and message in a compelling and connected way.
4. Stand for others in how you share your story.
5. Share your stories with kindness and love.

Remember, your story and message matter. There is a reason you are still here too. Be willing to share and give all you have been given to give and make the difference you are called to make in the world!

Maureen Famiano

Maureen Famiano is an award-winning media expert. She's been in the broadcast arena for more than thirty-five years as a television news reporter, producer, and executive producer. She began with a decade in New York as a reporter and then moved to Tampa Bay in 1996. She worked at NBC-WFLA for seventeen years as a news producer and then as executive producer of syndicated shows like *Daytime, Star Watch,* and *Reel Animals Fishing.* She was also an executive producer of the WTSP-CBS morning show *Great Day LIVE* for almost four years. In her time in morning-show television, she personally booked close to fifteen thousand guests on her shows.

She began her own company MEFMedia in 2019 after many guests wanted her help as a consultant to their businesses. Her company offers branding and strategies followed by creative ideas that get results and media attention with interviews. She works to pull the story out of a business, solopreneur, or individual to connect better with customers.

In 2020 and 2021, Maureen was nominated for the Best of the Bay in Tampa Bay marketing agencies and was awarded the Diwali recognition by the city of Hoboken as a champion of light and goodness. She has served as a community ambassador for the Super Bowl in Tampa, hosted TEDx Women Tampa in December 2021, and sat on the celebrity judges' panel for the American Lung Association's "Lip Sync for Lungs" event, as well as holding committee positions at the Centre Club, Tampa's premier business and social club. She began 2022 as a TEDx speaker in Tampa Bay in February.

www.MEFMedia.com
#togetherwewin
813-495-0663
Maureen Famiano & MEFMedia on Facebook
Maureen Famiano on LinkedIn

FIND YOUR MUHAMMAD ALI STRENGTH
BY ABBEY DAW

"Are you crazy?" asked my friend, her voice serious. "You just got laid off from your corporate job, and you're going to start a new business, now? In the middle of a pandemic? That's nuts, Abbey. No one does that."

But I did. I was tired of being afraid. This time, I listened to my deep soul calling. I took a breath—several actually—and decided to proceed forward.

I launched my business when many told me it was the wrong time. I launched my business when most would have run for safety. After having tremendous success as a teacher and leader in my community, I had just gotten laid off from my corporate job due to the pandemic. I was a mom of a precious, two-year-old girl. I had just secured low-income housing to face these tough times, and I was barely making that rent. What was I going to do now that I didn't even have a job? The responsible thing would have been to look for another nine-to-five job to make sure I could pay my bills. Many told me to do this and that it would be temporary and then I could follow my dreams "someday." Go for the safety and security, they said, but I felt otherwise.

I felt like I was sitting at a big game of chess. I was going to make the boldest move of my life when most weren't feeling brave at all. I was going to go for the big win, which was *disguised* as a big, fat death zone.

Yes, it was a risk and a big one. But I believed in taking risks. All the successful people I know often had to do this to get where they are today. So, I decided that this was the perfect opportunity to make my move and the risk of my life. **I wanted to be a leader again for women to do the same in their own lives. And I was so passionate about and believed in this work so strongly. I went for it.**

In the meantime, the pandemic continued. Stocks were falling. People were holed up in their homes, feeling breathless and powerless and afraid. Store shelves were empty, and people wouldn't look at each other in the grocery aisle. The fear was tangible.

I knew this fear. Despite all the amazing physical and leadership feats I'd accomplished in my lifetime. Meanwhile, I launched my new business despite the fear that sat restlessly in my body. The muffled voice of my soul somehow managed to override the terror that felt like a constant companion.

One evening, alone after my new business launch with zero sales coming in, I was sitting hunched on the floor of my shabby apartment while feeding my two-year-old mac and cheese out of a pan. I felt that huge wave of fear come over me. **This fear debilitated me, and I felt alone and vulnerable.**

I wanted to run for safety. The doubt of making the decision to follow my dreams had overtaken my body. Shit! I was in trouble and felt as though I was drowning and unable to catch my breath.

I would soon discover that having my breath alone made me the most abundant human alive. And I had been walking around holding my breath my entire life.

A tear dripped down my face, and I wiped it away quickly before my daughter could see it. I was doing everything I could to be the best mom, and I felt as if I had failed us both. As I was sitting in what felt like my own eye of the storm, I was living in my head, and the fear was winning, and I was no longer feeling my heart. My inner narrative was bullying me and was desperately urging me to go back to the daily machine of corporate life, working for the man that everyone seemed to be buying into and working at another purposeless job.

CONNECT WITH YOUR PURPOSE

My actual worst nightmare.

I kept telling myself, "Who are you to follow your dreams and live your purpose?" "You are an imposter." **I had completely forgotten who I was at that moment.**

I needed support, so I called one of my people. Make sure you have those people ready on speed dial, especially when you are going to follow your dreams—you are going to need them. These are your lifelines. These people are rare because they are the ones that tell you to keep going when you want to turn around and give up. Don't call those comfort seekers. Call on the brave ones. The ones that have already done what you want to do.

I knew the perfect person to talk to for advice. She was my warrior friend Vanessa and one of the strongest women alive. V started her own very successful business from scratch when she had absolutely nothing and many years later sold it to live a simpler life because she could; she had accomplished her dreams in business. Her business had changed lives. She never gave up, and she was living proof to me that when you keep suiting up and showing up, even when it gets freaking hard, miracles happen! I knew I could use her wisdom and guidance.

No matter how strong we are in life, it is important to lean on others and ask for help. **There is no weakness in being vulnerable; there is only strength. We all get scared. But it's what we do with the fear and how we respond to it that matters the most.** As I heard V's voice on the other end, I immediately felt held and understood in my fear. I continued to anxiously feed her all the evidence to believe that I was failing and I should give up, and my dreams did not matter.

As I was continuing to voice my fear, V generously interrupted me. "Abbey, I know you are scared, and I get it; I've been here repeatedly throughout my life." Then she went on to say, **"I want to tell you something that most won't tell you when starting and creating a business. It takes guts to follow our dreams, which is why most don't even entertain the idea."** Then with all her belief and strength of will learned through her lifetime, she added vehemently, **"It takes Muhammad Ali strength and the will to never give up on yourself and your desires in life!"**

I took a long pause, and then an exhale followed. I said, "Thank you. I am going to keep going." I understood what she meant.

I have learned that Muhammad Ali strength is that deeper, mighty force that you must tap into when the outside world is no longer giving you evidence that you should keep going. It's the strength that is hard to find. But it is the strength within that is so deep and has always been there for you from the moment you leave the womb and enter this world. **You must go there, and you must believe in yourself when nobody else does. Nobody is going to save you; you've got to save yourself. I knew that I had that strength because I had tapped into it many times before.**

This is the strength I tapped into when I was a young teenager when I wanted to die because I was gay and was living in my own hell of who I was. I was afraid I would go to hell if I came out as a gay woman because God wouldn't let gay people into heaven. This is what I was taught and believed, which is why I had so much fear in my little body. It has taken many years of unbecoming of who I was told I should be to become who I am deep inside. You have to disentangle the BS lies first, and you have to sit with the beast of fear and become its friend.

Anyways, back to Muhammad Ali strength.

It had once taken me Muhammad Ali strength to run eight marathons—some of the most prestigious in the world. It had once taken Muhammad Ali strength to get certified in this strange new thing called yoga in the western world in the nineties and then to teach thousands.

V simply reminded me that this was the strength that kept me alive when I felt the world was against me. This is the strength that is in you too. It is in all of us, and we must have a willingness to go deep down and find it. **The treasure is inside the body.** Vanessa gave me the one reminder that I needed. And from that moment forward, whenever I wanted to give up, I told myself to find my inner Muhammad Ali strength, and that is exactly what I did.

I kept going when fear told me to turn around and go back. Because of that, I suddenly was making more in my business than I did at my corporate job. I left the low-income housing with my daughter to a spacious and beautiful place we call home. From there, I film my courses and share my practice with extraordinary women from around the globe! Now, two years later, I am well on target to conquer all my lofty business goals. But more important to me is the impact I am having on women. By facing my fear, **I have now helped countless others reclaim their Magik in meditation, yoga, and especially reclaiming our breath and our lives—right in the midst of fear.**

You see, fear is not a fact; it's an energy that swallows us up in a false reality we have created in our minds to keep us safe.

One of my most influential teachers, Wim Hoff, is known for leading people through cold water therapy and ice baths to heal bodies and minds from life traumas. His work is powerful and has profoundly affected me on all levels.

His quote on fear changed my life the moment I read it: "Go to the fear, instead of the fear coming to you."

I discovered that if we go to our fear before it overtakes us, then the fear isn't that powerful. Really, give it a try. Today I have a weekly practice of sitting in five minutes of ice-cold baths to recalibrate my nervous system, and, in a lot of ways, this has saved my life. The cold water represents going to the fear and conquering it.

Once I put this into practice within my own life, I never experienced fear the same way again. **Now, whenever I smell fear, when it is close by, I make the decision to go to it.** I make the decision to camp out in what feels like the eye of the storm. Time and time again, I have made the decision that I befriend fear. I get to know it. By doing so, I have found that fear can be excitement for what is coming to you. By going to the fear, you dismantle its power over you. **In fact, going to the fear is liberating.** It's a place that most run from. We do everything in our power to resist fear, to fight it off, to stay safe. Yet, when you make the decision to go to the fear and meet up with it, you find that it isn't as scary after all. On the other side of that fear are the most beautiful and exquisite views you will ever see in your life. Fear is the door to freedom and transformation.

When you sense fear is nearby, get excited. This is your opportunity to grow and become braver. This is an indication that your life is about to change and that, on the other side, it is a gift for your life. If you can do this, your life will never be the same.

Look around you. We need brave souls to have a willingness to go into the places few dare to go because these are the next innovators and creators of our new world. These are the leaders and those that will give us hope for blue skies ahead.

Tips on going to fear and following your big life purpose:

- **Go to the fear.**

When you feel like fear is close by, go to it by feeling it. Sit with it, no distractions, and breathe into it. Breathe into it until it starts to have less power over you. Talk to it and ask it what its message is for you and decide for yourself if this message is even true. Let your little inner self know that everything is going to be okay. Remember that 99 percent of what we worry about doesn't come true.

- **Write down your fears.**

Journaling what is on your mind dismantles the fear once you get it on paper and out of your head. When we read what we have written down, it makes the fear less powerful. Even five to ten minutes of daily journaling practice will do wonders for your life. Get it out of your body and look at it. It's another way to go to the fear instead of letting it come to you.

- **Create a weekly or even daily meditation practice.**

Sitting in quiet for even five minutes a day while taking deep breaths will significantly improve your life in ways that you can't even imagine. Your breath is your access to your superpower. When you sit in the quiet and ask your body a question, the body will give you an answer. You are no longer wrestling with the ego, which is fear-based and comes from the spiraling of the monkey mind. The body has the answers; go inside and get them.

- **It's not about perfection; it is about consistency.**

Give yourself grace. This fear muscle must be exercised daily and isn't going to get better overnight. Practice observing the fear and making a different thought choice at that moment. This is about suiting up and showing up! It does get better. Remember, though, sometimes it must get worse before it gets better. Don't get discouraged. Just keep going. Remember to tap into your Muhammad Ali strength.

- **Love your life now.**

When you love yourself fully, your body doesn't have time to feel the fear. Fear can't co-exist when you feel all the love. Love is much bigger than your fear. Learn to love your life right now, at this moment, without any circumstances to change. You can always notice what you have instead of what you don't have. When we do this and breathe, we have everything we ever need. Right now.

- **And lastly, have gratitude.**

Live in gratitude daily, and fear will never take over you again. Have gratitude for it all. One of my greatest teachers Gabby Bernstein taught me to "faith it until I make it." I have discovered through her teachings that obstacles are opportunities, and detours take you in the right direction. Celebrate it all.

In summary, step into your purpose and decide to take back your life. Take your life pen back from whomever you have given it to and rewrite your next chapter! Be the hero of your own story and sit in all the eyes of your storms, riding each one out because on the other side of those storms are the most beautiful views you will ever see, that few will dare to ever see in their lifetime. And while you are at it, don't forget to breathe. A deeper breath means a deeper life. You are bold, strong, and capable.

Abbey Daw

Abbey Daw has been teaching for eighteen years in various studios throughout Utah. She is a registered 200-hour, 500-hour yoga instructor and a 300-hour registered yoga therapist. Abbey has also trained with Ana Forrest and completed her advanced training in New York in 2013. She is an entrepreneur at heart and won entrepreneur of the year in 2015 for the Salt Lake City women's business center for her first business, Sweat & Soul. She is currently the founder of "The Magik Experience Membership," which is an online community that empowers women to embody their light and live their purposes through her transformational breath and meditation exercises. She loves to mentor and coach women on their journey to embodiment and finding their purpose. Abbey is also an attuned Reiki practitioner and loves to help women heal in order to live a life full of joy. Abbey's most important job is being a mother to her daughter, Mae, and in her spare time, she enjoys mountain biking, listening to music, drinking coffee, and being in the great outdoors. She is currently writing a book and aspires to be an author and speaker, traveling the world to inspire others to live a happy and healthy life full of Magik!

abbeydaw@gmail.com
(801) 671-9831
www.abbeydaw.com
Facebook: facebook.com/abbey.daw.3
Instagram: @abbeydaw

STEPPING INTO YOUR SOUL'S PURPOSE
BY SAM YAU

What is soul?

Why do we need to connect to our soul to find our highest purpose?

Our soul is that divine spark that was planted deep inside us that is already connected to the source. Our soul helps us to remember our divine origin pin this human incarnation. It guides us in our evolution to the highest consciousness and returning to our source.

Our soul is our true but veiled identity. The essence of our soul is love, reflecting the essence of the Divine, which is love.

Our ego is the gift of self-image that our mind creates to help us to survive and thrive in the harsh human realities. It is a construction, and therefore, not real. But it is a useful device that is centered on the survival of the "me."

Let's distinguish ego from egoistic. Ego is the image of self that is created by our mind to navigate this human reality. Being egoistic is the stage of ego development when it stays mostly self-centered. The egoistic does not care for others initially. But it can be instructed by our "soul" to extend the circle of care to family, to friends, to communities, to nations, to humanity, to animal and plant kingdoms, to Gaia, and to the entire cosmos. This is the journey of the heart.

The ego is our identity when we are only conscious of our humanity. The generic purpose for an incarnated soul is to become aware of its true identity as a soul. In the process of spiritual growth, we shift our identity to our soul and surrender our ego in service to our soul's purpose.

Embracing Our Uniqueness

Each of us is unique in the way we are human, in the way we are divine, and in the way they blend together in us. We celebrate the glorious diversity in all creations while being aware of our underlying sameness in our divine spark.

In the individuation of the ego, we synthesize our life experiences. We absorb expectations from our parents, from our church, from our school, from our friends and communities. Such became the substances for the ego to form our sense of self and our life's purpose.

But the soul's purpose comes from a deeper origin. It is why we are here in the first place, even though we have no memory of it. It is carried in our energy field, and it will call on us from our subjective inner world that only we can know.

A shift is necessary from conformity to outside expectations to our soul's invitation from the inside. Embracing our uniqueness means we are totally free to create our life and answer the call from our souls.

Here is a quote from my poem "Soul's Journey" that shares how unique and beautiful you are:

*You surge
from the ocean of awareness
as a desire of the Divine
to experience Itself as the unique you:
one strand of the infinite glory
and variety of Its creations.
You are a wave rising up to
the beautiful dance of life,
remerging into eternity.*

If the generic purpose of a soul is to learn to love in a deeper way in our human journey, then there is always a specific way we can serve fellow human beings. Our unique life experiences create our unique gifts for us to serve the world.

How Soul's Purpose is Revealed to Us

Our soul guides our journey by speaking to us as our inner voice. No one else can hear it. There will not be a witness. We must learn to hear it alone and trust it with increasing confidence as part of our spiritual growth.

There will be synchronicities from our outer realities to validate our strengthening conviction from within. We can ask our soul for synchronicities and signs. Our soul has the superpower of the Divine to manifest outer realities to confirm our inner intuition.

Our purpose in life evolves over time based on the level of consciousness we have attained. Each of the stages of evolution is also according to an original blueprint of our soul's journey. An earlier purpose serves a subsequent purpose until we reach our highest purpose in this lifetime. There can be many detours when we are unable or unwilling to hear the calling of our soul, which is patient and persistent.

Sometimes, we feel we have lost our way. We could not find meaning and purpose. We feel abandoned and lose our faith in the Divine. Such darkness is often called the dark night of the soul.

We might experience a major trauma with debilitating emotional effects. We seem to be stalled in pain with no ability to move forward. Know that our trauma is often a doorway to our awakening to our soul. Our grief opens our hearts to the suffering of the world. Our wounding becomes the catalyst for the emergence of our calling.

How It Feels When We Are Aligned with Our Soul's Purpose

The sense of finding the meaning of our life is palpable and unmistakable. There is a sense of deep peace that resembles the feeling of being at home at last. A purposeful determination is often accompanied by a fiery passion. The joy is organic and visceral, as work is no longer work but a labor of love. It is neither a job nor a career. It is a calling that uplifts our spirit.

My Story of Finding My Soul's Purpose

I have reinvented my life several times, from a six-month baby on a refugee boat, to a penniless student from a distant land to the CEO of a billion-dollar corporation, to the chairman of an iconic pioneer growth center, to a poet of who writes about soul's journey, life's vicissitudes, trauma and healing, consciousness, and mysticism.

Here is a brief account of how I answered the call of my soul to be a poet.

In 2016, my son Ryan killed himself with a bullet through his brain.

The moment I heard the news, I knew my life was changed forever.

To grieve, I retreated into seclusion. All my interests at that time dropped away.

For more than twenty years, I have been on a journey of personal and spiritual growth. I always knew that I am a spirit. With Ryan's death, and my desire to be close to him, simply knowing that I am a soul was no longer enough.

One day, a question was stuck in my mind that would not go away. What if I live as a soul in human clothes rather than as a human who has soul? That pondering set in motion a startling inversion of priority. Asking my soul that question with persistence and commitment catapulted me into a surprising journey that I could not have imagined just a few years ago.

I received clear messages from Ryan and two world-renowned mediums to write poems. I was told I would be a healer in words. That was unfathomable to me. I was neither a wordsmith nor a healer. I had never written a serious poem in my life. But my soul's whisper was unceasing. Within a few months, through a series of synchronicities, a poetry coach, an amazing artist to illustrate my poems, and many new friends became the angels in my poetry journey. The calling was unmistakable. I surrendered.

My verses, together with love from my friends and family, have healed me. My poetic musings clarified, distilled, deepened, and ingrained the essence of past spiritual experiences onto my being. As I sculpted my poems, my poems were sculpturing me at the same time. Writing poetry has become a most joyous and uplifting spiritual practice for me.

The soul's journey is one that discovers the true nature of the Divine, and each soul is love itself. Peeling off all layers of reality, only awareness and love remain.

My poems have healed and transformed me; by sharing them, I hope they will heal and inspire others.

I continue to all my purpose to guide and brighten forth the healing words I'm called to bring to the world.

Purpose Can Be a State of Being, Not Necessarily What We Do

Over the years, everything I did was fading away in their significance. It was the predominant feeling and my state of being during that period that now stays front and center in my awareness.

Was I feeling loving and being loved in my life? Did I love myself? Did I love in my interactions with my family and friends and fellow human beings in all other spheres of my life?

The cosmic design of the soul's journey in the human world is to evolve and grow our capacity to expand our hearts to be more loving and expand our minds to be inclusive.

What we do is merely a training vehicle for evolving and becoming who we are. From the perspective of the soul, an accomplishment-oriented purpose is a transitional purpose for us to finally reach a soul-based purpose.

I end this chapter by sharing with you a poem of mine that illuminates some of the points above in finding our soul's purpose:

DO NOT LET ANYONE TELL YOU TO LIVE SOMEONE ELSE'S LIFE

Do not let anyone tell you to live someone else's life.
You have a gift to co-create your special life with the Divine.
Let the spark in you shine, live and dance like a unique spirit.
Shape your inner world with qualities that bring you delight.
Live inside out, the outside world will coalesce into your design.
Do not let anyone tell you to live someone else's life.

Listen to your inner voice from your soul and let it guide you, trust it.
Living the authentic you will bring you freedom and joy, claim it.
Let the spark in you shine, live and dance like a unique spirit.

You are a soul incarnated in the human school to learn to love,
You are frozen light that soon will take the soaring flight.
Do not let anyone tell you to live someone else's life.

Already connected to The Source, turn it on and drink it in.
Angels are always there to help if you let your intuition align.
Let the spark in you shine, live and dance like a unique spirit.

You have been knocking at the door from the inside all your life.
Turn around, you are perfect and totally lovable, live it.
Do not let anyone tell you to live someone else's life.
Let the spark in you shine, live and dance like a unique spirit.

Sam Yau

Sam Yau is a retired business executive, splitting his time between managing his investments and writing poetry.

Sam has reinvented his life several times, from a six-month-old baby on a refugee boat, to a penniless student from a distant land, to the CEO of a billion-dollar corporation, to the chairman of a well-known center for personal growth, to a poet who writes about the soul's journey, life's vicissitudes, trauma and healing, consciousness, science and spirituality, and mysticism.

Sam holds an MBA in finance from the University of Chicago. Sam is a single parent living with his fourteen-year-old daughter in Laguna Beach. Sam enjoys music, hiking, and active travel around the world.

Email: cyyau1@gmail.com

GRIEF: A CATALYST AND OPPORTUNITY FOR POSITIVE CHANGE
BY JANET SCHMIDT

On March 8, 2019, just two days after Lent began, at eighty years old, my dad died of congestive heart failure and cancer. On February 17, 2021, Ash Wednesday, my mom died of "failure to thrive" at the age of seventy-eight. During the two years after Dad died, Mom was lost and sad. She was also angry. On March 26, 2021, my mother-in-law died in her sleep at the age of ninety-one.

I remember the day Dad passed away. I was in the room with Mom. After Dad had died, I told Mom I thought Dad was gone. She walked over to his bed and took his pajama top in her hands, and said, while angrily pulling on his top, "You promised me I would go first! You promised me."

I absolutely believe she died of a failure to thrive because she had no desire to go on without Dad. She refused to go to the doctor; she refused to let me in the house for a visit some days arguing that "you know why" when I didn't have a clue, and she rarely left the house having her groceries and medication delivered. She lived in the same home she had lived with Dad since the 1980s. And that is exactly where I found her, lying on the floor semi-conscious. My mom gave up, let the grief fester inside her, and finally, it destroyed her will to live and thrive. Finding my mother on the floor semi-conscious will stick in my mind forever, and I still feel a small bit of guilt for not going to visit her sooner that week. I think the "what ifs" will haunt me for a while.

When my mother-in-law died, I felt very sad because I hadn't really seen her except on Zoom for family events since the pandemic. She lived in a nursing home in the same town my husband's sister and we lived. My husband had seen her a few days before she died. She was a gentle and kind person. She always told me she loved me at the end of each and every phone call we had. That's the crux of the matter: I didn't get to tell her I loved her before she died, and that hurt.

The emotions involved in dealing with the deaths of both my parents and mother-in-law are difficult to articulate in words, and nothing I can say will do any real justice to the experience. I will admit the period of my father's illness from 2013 to his death in 2019 was without question the most difficult thing I have ever personally gone through. So many things that seemed so difficult in the past now seem nothing in comparison to the death of my parents. So far, not one day has gone by that I don't think about Dad, Mom, or my mother-in-law, and some days, the pain feels as raw and fresh as if it just happened a few days ago. We all know our time is limited on this earth, but this truth tends to hit you hard when death touches us personally. Sometimes I feel a wave of "this can't be real," like I really can't believe it happened. The fact that you will never see this person you have lost in the flesh or ever hug them again is really hard to process on an emotional level, regardless of how much time passes.

Grief can push you into a place that you would not normally go willingly. To really make change significantly for the better and to make the painful decisions required of living life as we really want to live it, we often have to **get down deep into the crap that has built up over the duration of our lives**, those static feelings of anger, guilt, shame, regret, fear, sadness, betrayal, and self-disgust. The trick to this is whether we decide to stay and face it or continue to deny this part of ourselves and let it continue to fester.

Since I had personally seen the results of not facing those feelings, I decided to face my demons. There is no doubt a lot of pain is residing there, and going voluntarily to face it is not an easy choice to make. It was unpleasant, to say the least, and there were days I wanted to run the other way. But, I managed to work through a lot of my own "stuff," and while I am not sure if I am past all of it, I did enough work to allow me to move further than I ever had previously. Some of that emotional "corruption" I had carried around for years had permanently cleared. After this, I felt comfortable giving myself some grace and breathing room. I felt a lightness inside of me that I had never felt before. I felt almost giddy. For a time, everything seemed so much brighter and exhilarating.

Grief can be a very powerful agent of change because it offers us a chance to experience immense personal growth if we choose to let it happen. Unpleasant times can truly help us carve out a path to our own happiness and purpose. The key is we must be **active participants in directing our positive change**. It does not happen passively. If you make it your goal to clarify your desires and build the life you want to live, you are making the experience of grief work for you. I have also discovered the more smoothly we handle the countless number of challenges in our life, the better off we will be. Feeling bad as I did, I ended up feeling very motivated to do all I could to make myself feel better. I knew I would always carry the loss of my parents and mother-in-law with me. My goal was not to totally rid myself of any feelings of sorrow because sorrow is part of what we experience in life as human beings.

For the first time in my life, I was able to **take the time to examine my options for making positive changes** and not just think about them in an off-hand way. During this time of reflection, I tried to keep true to the core of who I am. **I realized I had gotten so off-track in my life that I felt like I was no longer someone I could recognize. I had lost my way and was adrift without a real purpose in life.** While I hope I continue to live a healthy life, who knows what is in store for me. I realized that time was short, and I was already in my sixties. **I made the decision to follow my dreams now because later may not come.**

I knew that I had always wanted to leave something good behind for others, a legacy of some sort. I asked myself, what do I want to do with the rest of my life? During my reflection on that question, I remembered my life-long love of writing and how good I felt doing it. One of my old dreams had been to have my writing published. Why couldn't I do that now? There was no reason for not reaching for that goal. I could become a published author and do something I loved to do at the same time! The opportunity to become a published author came my way earlier this year, and I said yes to that opportunity fearlessly. This chapter is the result of that opportunity. I wanted my family, friends, and anyone who may read it to know that grief is a natural process in life that we all will experience. We can take that grief and make something good of it, like this chapter I've written, or we can let it fester and destroy us. I feel that this was the right choice for me, and I hope that what I have written touches a chord in others to find or align with their true purpose. I also have a novel in the process of being self-published as well, and that's what I really want to do for the rest of my life. Reach out to others through the written word. Make them cry, laugh, never give up, and contemplate life's crazy ups and downs. I personally feel my soul is lighter, and I'm stronger now that I am using my gift of writing in a positive and purposeful way.

What type of writing did I want to do? I felt I wanted to inspire and connect with others. I want to help others believe in themselves and to help them discover that they have personal power residing inside of them, just like I do. I want to help them develop confidence in who they are and that they can resolve problems. They can become resilient enough to bounce back from life's challenges. They can manifest the belief and own the responsibility for transforming and moving forward in life. I realized my anxiety about the future began to fade the more I got clear on what I needed and wanted to happen in my life. **I found I became more confident in making choices that would bring me forward from where I was to where I wanted to be. I stopped worrying about what other people thought of me or my choices.** In the end, it's my life, and as long as I am comfortable with my decisions, that is all that matters.

I decided to **make my happiness a priority** as well because I deserve happiness and joy in my life. I realized happiness was something that could be crafted through intentional choices and that I needed to work on my perspective and mindset. I needed to **surround myself with a support group of people who are of like mind, encouraging, and positive**. Networking is an excellent way to find people that are supportive and positive.

Grief can be a driving force to benefit others or to make the world a better place. A case in point: on December 14, 2012, at Sandy Hook Elementary School, a gunman opened fire on students and faculty in Newtown, Connecticut. At the end of his shooting spree, he had killed twenty children and six educators.

Scarlett Lewis' six-year-old son Jesse was killed in his first-grade classroom when gunman Adam Lanza opened fire at Sandy Hook Elementary. She wasn't surprised to hear from police officers who told her that her son had reportedly helped save other children's lives in the last moments of his own. Jesse yelled for his classmates to run during a short pause in the shooting. Several students heeded his call and were able to escape.

Inspired by her son's compassion and courage, Lewis created the Jesse Lewis Choose Love Movement. "I thought, if he could face the shooter and tell his friends to run if he could do that in the face of complete horror, I can certainly get up every day and promote a message of choosing love." The Jesse Lewis Choose Love Movement is a charitable organization that focuses on empowering children by making sure they have access to social and emotional learning, or SEL, in their schools and communities.

The core values for Jesse Lewis Choose Love Movement are based around "nurturing, healing, love"—three words Jesse had written on the kitchen chalkboard (phonetically spelled) before his death. Scarlett explains the organization's goal as "teaching kids how to have positive relationships, how to label and manage their emotions, coping, and resilience. Basically, how to feel kindness, caring, and concern for themselves and others. Responsible decision-making."

As I have moved through my healing and stepped more into my purpose by choosing to have joy, happiness, and contentment, I find that I am more **grateful for all the good things I have in my life**. I realize even more so that many of the issues that crop up in life are nothing compared to what some other people go through. Grief has given me more compassion for myself and others. I now have a thicker skin that will serve me well for the rest of my life.

This reminds me of one more thing that I believe is central to becoming a mature adult. Resiliency. Resiliency is having strong inner conviction and self-confidence in your own worth, values, and judgments. You do not feel the need to depend upon the approval or disapproval of others to determine the course of your life. Resiliency develops if you are able to use **adversity as an intermediary to positive and transformative change**. With resiliency, you will have the capacity to recover quickly from whatever life may throw at you and come out of it stronger and tougher than you were before.

No matter what challenging situation we may be facing, whether it is mourning the loss of a loved one, a divorce, money problems, or the million other things life can throw at us, **there is always an opportunity for positive change**. Adversity in any form, which includes grief, can be a catalyst for positive change. The more adverse the situation, the more opportunities for positive growth are available.

Tips to Choosing Positive Growth:

1. Go deep and face your feelings.
2. Extend others and yourself grace.
3. Realign with your purpose.
4. Choose to bring love and joy into your life.
5. Choose to be grateful.
6. Remember to use adversity as an opportunity for positive change. Choose to follow your dreams.
7. Choose to be resilient when facing life's challenges.

Janet L. Schmidt

Janet L. Schmidt is the author of the chapter "Grief: A Catalyst and Opportunity for Positive Change" in the book *Step into Your Brilliant Purpose*. This chapter is born from personal life experience and her strong desire to help others. Currently, Janet is working on finishing her first book, *As You Love Yourself: A Journey to Self-Awareness*, which she hopes to launch in 2022. For a year and a half, she was a freelance writer for a local urban women's magazine and wrote features on businesses in the community. Janet has always had a passion for writing. As a child, she would sit outside and spend hours writing stories and poems. She is the mother of two adult children and has been married thirty-two years to her husband, Lyle.

Facebook: https://www.facebook.com/janets1111
Twitter: @JanetLSchmidt2
LinkedIn: https://www.linkedin.com/in/janet-schmidt-44868833/

CHOOSE TO FULLY LIVE
BY S. DAWN BRADFORD

I spent my life avoiding pain. I stayed safe and small, mired in depression and anxiety. I hurt people in my attempt not to be hurt. I lashed out at others and then complained that no one loved me. Chronic health problems compounded my isolation.

I may have stayed stuck in this pattern except that my health problems worsened. The paralytic attacks that had been in remission for several years came back with a vengeance, occurring almost daily. My muscles weakened within a matter of weeks, and I became an invalid.

The loss of my mobility was devastating, and doctors told me that I would be in and out of the wheelchair for the rest of my life due to a neuromuscular disorder. I was thirty-nine and had put off enjoying life until it was too late. In that moment of understanding, I gave up.

My health declined rapidly. I felt death creeping along my bones, stealing away my life. I made peace with the process and welcomed it, causing an argument with my husband. He felt I was going to get better, but I knew I was dying. I agreed to go to a holy man, knowing that he would help my husband see the truth. Instead, I was told it was not my time to die. It didn't make me feel hopeful; it made me angry. I didn't want to live.

Traditional medicine could do nothing for me, so to appear to keep fighting, I turned to alternative medicine. The doctor calmly listened to what I had to say and then began his exam. He paused, looked at me, and said, "Your organs are trying to shut down."

I replied, "I know." He didn't argue or try to convince me that I didn't feel what was happening inside my own body. He listened to me and my body, giving words to what I felt inside.

At the end of the initial consultation, he said, "I can't do anything about the paralytic attacks, but I can get you out of the wheelchair."

I decided that if I had to live, I was going to do it standing up. My husband drove me twice a week to my appointments, and I began to get stronger. I drank nasty green health drinks and made lifestyle changes. Within a year, I no longer needed the wheelchair at home, only when I went out. My recovery was slow, even after my paralytic attacks went back into remission, but I became a success story.

I stepped into health with daily gratitude for the ability to walk, clean my house, and drive. I looked to the future with hope-filled eyes, not understanding that my physical journey was merely false labor pains to the true labor only a breath away.

A vague disquiet gnawed at me. I tried to ignore it, but the feeling grew, demanding attention. I will never forget the moment I broke through the amnesia hiding my past and discovered that the worst possible thing I could imagine happening to a child had happened to me. My life suddenly, tragically made sense.

Pain and memories flooded in, and my life ground to a halt while I tried desperately to keep my head above water. Memories surfaced in waves, slamming into me and then receding, giving me enough time to gasp for air before the next arrived.

I began to see my abusers' fingerprints all over my life. My choices, my reactions, what I liked and disliked, all traced back to the severe child abuse I had suffered. I lost my sense of self.

Each successive memory was more horrific than the last, making me sure I had uncovered the worst of the abuse, but the depravity of my abusers exceeded my imagination.

The uninformed told me it was better not to remember. After all, my brain was protecting me. But the hidden cancer of my abuse had slowly poisoned me for years, and I refused to give any more of my life to my abusers. The only way to be free was to fully experience the pain, the anger, and the truth of my childhood.

When new memories came up, I instinctively fought against the process because it hurts. The longer I fought the process, the more it hurt. I learned to allow my memories to surface and not push away whatever feelings accompanied them. However, I didn't push to remember any more than I needed to for healing.

I attended therapy. I learned about healthy boundaries and began enforcing them in my life. I learned how to release my pain and anger in healthy ways and moved from victim to survivor. I grew out of my therapist and found another who specialized in trauma.

Little by little, I began to discover a world outside I never imagined existed. By feeling the pain and anger, I opened up the possibility to feel joy and contentment. One day I went for a walk, something I had been too unhealthy to do most of my adult life. I noticed the beauty of the world around me for the first time. I had viewed the world through a fuzzy black and white lens that had been removed to reveal the world in vivid color.

I wasn't able to stay in that beautiful place, but once I caught a glimpse of it, I understood what I was fighting for. I became more willing to walk through the darkness to come out into the light.

My healing journey wasn't quick, and it wasn't easy. I was diagnosed with dissociative identity disorder, previously known as multiple personality disorder, which felt as devastating to me as my physical diagnosis had been. The dissociated parts of my personality, or alters, had worked together to make sure both those around me and I didn't know I was multiple in order to keep me safe. With the return of my memories, the child alters that had lain dormant for years began surfacing, even coming out in public.

At first, I hated my alters. They were strange, and I wanted them to go away and leave me alone. The more I fought them, the more they plagued me. There was no escape from people who lived inside my own brain. I had to learn to work with them. As I began to listen to my alters and their stories, I realized that they are all parts of me without the vast experience I have gained over the course of my life. There were valid reasons why their belief systems and coping mechanisms were so different from my own.

I learned that my disorder was a gift of protection against abuse so severe my brain chose to fracture to survive. My therapist helped me understand my alters were trying to protect me in the best way they knew how. I began approaching them with love and understanding, and we worked together to meet our shared goals.

I discovered I had within me vigilantes, rebels, and doormats. There were frightened children, know-it-alls, and those who believed I deserved the abuse. The more I accepted and communicated with them, the more I became co-conscious, meaning that I shared my headspace with one or more alters when they were in control. I felt what they felt; I knew what they knew. This allowed me to step into a life experience and viewpoint foreign to me. My compassion grew not only for myself but for others.

We all have different parts. The side that loves to party, the one who talks nonsense to babies, and the part that insists we get our work done. The difference is that you can choose when and where you step into these different aspects of your personality, and I can't, though I have learned to manage it. I learned I am both compassionate and judgmental. I am a strong woman and a scared girl. I am a victim and a survivor.

I could not step into an empowered life filled with purpose until I accepted all the parts of myself, both present and past, good and bad. Acceptance could not happen without remembering. Remembering could not happen without being willing to feel pain. Being present in my life showed me how my suffering had hurt my family and created chaos. I accepted responsibility and began changing my interactions. By doing these things, I freed my energy and my soul, which allowed me to step into a new life. I started saying yes to each opportunity that came up. I learned how to write well, which led to writing my memoir and becoming a writing coach. I began running production on writing retreats and conferences, which took me to Scotland. I became a life coach and began mentoring survivors of abuse. When the 2020 pandemic shut down the world, I used that time to complete my business degree. Each time, I began with a simple desire to pursue something that I was passionate about.

Most people don't have to confront the many aspects of their past and personality in the way that I did. But at the core of my experience, I am not so different from you, for pain is a part of the human experience. We all hold deep hurt within us, things we don't know if it is possible to heal from. I managed to push my pain down for thirty years until I became too weak and was forced to face it.

I got to the place where I am because each day, I chose to live instead of die, and then I did whatever it took to get through that day. On my good days, I searched for answers, and the universe put books, ideas, and people in my path to help me along my journey. On my bad days, I kept breathing through the pain.

There are bits of every emotion and every personality inside us. Without acceptance, we are divided within ourselves. When we refuse to accept a part of ourselves, it rears its ugly head. When we accept and give our feelings a voice, peace and unity enter.

In that space of acceptance, I began to live in the present and experience the unique joy of each moment. I strive to capture as many of those moments as I can because it was worth every bit of hard work and pain to feel alive. I believe that joy and pain are connected. Numbing the pain numbs the joy.

What is joy? To me, it is living at peace with myself and those around me and deeply experiencing the present moment. When I became truly present in my life, my relationships blossomed, opportunities abounded, and joy exploded.

I see the walking dead all around me, but people cross my path who are ready to wake up, feel their pain, and learn how to feel joy. My message to them is simple—it doesn't matter what you have gone through, how horrible your past or present, healing is possible. The universe is guiding you to a beautiful place if you are brave enough to try and not give up.

You have to want a new life so desperately that you are willing to see the truth about yourself and your past, be willing to feel whatever pain and anger surfaces, and step into change. I never lie and tell people it will be easy, but it is worth the journey.

The path forward is full of seemingly opposing ideas. Increasing our capacity to feel pain increases our capacity to feel joy. Being vulnerable brings strength. Accepting the darkest parts of ourselves allows our unique gifts to shine and benefit those around us.

I don't seek after or welcome pain. Even now, after so much practice, I still resist the process. But allowing the pain to coexist within me darkens my view, shrinks my life, and blocks my progress. I no longer accept that way of life, so I allow the pain to surface, I feel it, and I learn from it. Only then does it pass beyond me. The world becomes bright and beautiful again, and I move forward with the goals I have.

If you want to experience greater joy and opportunities in your life, begin today.

1. Be Still:

Constant activity and noise in our lives help us avoid our emotions. Routinely take the time to stop and listen to what your mind and body are trying to tell you. Notice.

Pay attention to what sensations you feel in your body. We call them feelings because we physically feel them.

2. Identify:

Name the emotion you feel.

3. Express:

Allow the emotion to flow over you without judgment. Feelings are not good or bad; they are simply communication.

If you have routinely repressed your emotions, you will need an action in order to feel your emotion. Punch a pillow, watch a sad movie, or talk to someone you trust. Write or draw out your feelings—anything that helps you express your emotion in a healthy way that doesn't hurt yourself or others.

4. Visualize:
Imagine the emotion you are dealing with by giving it a shape and a color.[1] Visualize it in front of you. There is no right or wrong here—allow your imagination free reign.

5. Let go:
Invite your deity or higher power to come and give the shape you created to them or destroy it by throwing it into the sun or imagining some other destructive power. Your brain is creative and unique; let it handle this however works for you.

6. Refill:
When we let something go, we create space within ourselves. That bit of emptiness is uncomfortable. Don't leave it empty, or you will fill it back up with the same emotion. Fill it with positive energy and personal power. If you imagined a higher power, receive a gift in exchange for what you gave. Identify what it is and why it has meaning to you.

As you practice feeling your emotions, you will begin to identify what needs healing within you, whether it is physical, emotional, or spiritual. Dig down to what causes you the most personal pain, and then seek answers for how to heal. Be aware of what opens up to you, even if it seems unrelated. Then remain patient but persistent.

Your new path might be hard, or it might feel easier because others come into your life to help you along your way. Just remember, keep getting through each hard day, use your good days for gratitude and guidance, and don't give up.

Once you feel the difference of what a life fully lived feels like, you will never settle for mediocrity again. You can choose to live a purpose-driven and joyful life—one breath and one feeling at a time.

---

[1] Robinson, Pam (2022, March 1). Integrative Processing Technique. Retrieved from Institute of Healing Arts: https://www.ihaofutah.com/integrative-processing-technique.

S. Dawn Bradford

S. Dawn Bradford is a life coach, international public speaker, and presenter sharing the message of hope that healing is possible no matter what we have experienced in our lives. She empowers abuse survivors through workshops, coaching, and a private Facebook group. Dawn successfully manages dissociative identity disorder and works to destigmatize it through speaking openly about the challenges and triumphs of working together with her alters/parts as well as mentoring others with the disorder.

Dawn is a writing coach and the event production supervisor at Calliope Writing Coach, has written guest blogs for the American SPCC, and appeared in two self-help books on depression and healing. She loves to hike in the mountains around her Utah home with her dog, Ginger, and cook for her kids (or chat while her husband cooks.)

To learn more about her journey of healing both mind and body battered by severe childhood abuse, read her memoir, *Broken No More: A True Story of Abuse, Amnesia, and Finding God's Love.*

    sdawnbradford@gmail.com
    801-574-8260
    www.sdawnbradford.com
    facebook.com/sdawnbradford
    Twitter: @sdawnbradford
    YouTube: S. Dawn Bradford
    Instagram: @sdawnbradford

SECTION 2:

Step into Your Brilliant Purpose

SHINE IN YOUR PURPOSE!
BY MAUREEN RYAN BLAKE

It is funny the path we are on. We are always moving, sometimes forward, often backward, and at moments, it feels like we are standing still. But in all of it, we are moving on the road of our purpose.

I am grateful I always knew I had a purpose, something I was called to do, somewhere I was meant to go, someplace I was searching to call home. And equipped with drive and determination, I set out to make a difference for others and stand in my legacy.

I was never afraid of change. I was born in Brooklyn, New York, and have called home to Fort Lauderdale, Chicago, Colorado Springs, San Diego, and now Little Rock. For me, moving was always an adventure, packing, preparing, but most of all, the planning was my favorite part. I loved the excitement and newness of moving to a new place held.

Tip 1

Something I learned that helped me get settled after moving: When you arrive, make your bed first. There is a comfort in knowing you have one place you can lay your head when it is time to sleep and close your eyes; everything else falls into place.

Following the move to San Diego in fall 2011, I found myself lonely and not sure of who I was. I knew I had to make a change.

It was the week of my birthday, my husband was away on business, and the highlight of my day was going to be waiting for my best friend from New York City to call. With that realization, something stirred in me. I decided I was not going to spend my birthday alone. At that moment, I decided I would create my own birthday celebration.

With courage, I approached a fellow kindergarten mom. I asked her if she would like to join me for my birthday celebration; this year, I was throwing my own party. This former model and TV celebrity said yes and became a life-long friend and first member of The Power of the Tribe. Over the course of the next ten years, other women joined our group, and we shared many a girls' nights out, memories, love, and support. Each of us brought something unique and valuable to the group. It was something special, and we knew it.

Tip 2

If you are feeling lonely and looking for connection and community, be willing to reach out and invite others to connect with you.

Being grateful for my tribe, I started The Power of the Tribe online community to serve other female entrepreneurs who, through divorce, death, childbirth, moving, or other events in life, lost their identity and their joy. What I learned about the power of women was we are better together.

Tip 3

If you are looking to connect with other women, focus outward and serve. When you are vulnerable, open, loving, and giving, you will attract other amazing women and form your own power group. Magic will happen when you connect with others, with no expectation, and from a place of generosity. The secret is all in your state of being. Give, and you will receive.

Being open to change, there were many plans I created for my purpose. I planned to be a big musician, always on stage, singing out my heart and soul for all the world to hear. I planned to be an eloquent professor, sharing the joy and love of history for the world to remember and take notice. What I discovered was I was an entrepreneur, always ready to build, plan, and create the next great thing.

Tip 4

It is okay to try different careers and paths just keep moving. Change is not the enemy but can often lead to great discoveries. Denying your gifts and living without love and passion is the source of discontent and can lead to an unhappy life.

Early on in my journey, I committed to being a lifelong learner. As a scholar of history, I looked at life as a great big tapestry. Always applying new pieces of knowledge like pieces of cloth. And for each new item learned, a new piece of the tapestry became a unique square, adding value to the whole as the tapestry expanded and grew.

Finding one's purpose is a lot like the pieces of knowledge that make up the tapestry of life. You add experiences, relationships, and achievements as you continue your journey. And it is not the number of items you accumulate that counts for happiness, but the collective whole that makes up the journey. Knowing one's purpose can take time, can change, and is not always clear. This may be frustrating, and that is okay. But just like the tapestry, it is the creativity, the planning, the failing that make up a fulfilled and happy life.

Tip 5

Hold space for yourself as you continue uncovering your purpose. Be kind to yourself and remember to celebrate the wins.

So, where does our purpose come from? I believe we are all born with our purpose, a divine mission that was clustered in our DNA. A purpose so special, only you can fulfill. And within our purpose, we are connected like a web of energy, each adding and sourcing our highest energy, a contribution to the greater good we all share.

To stand in our purpose, we must vibrate at the highest frequencies of human behavior, love, gratitude, and generosity. On that same note, when burdened with doubt, fear, greed, and hate, one's purpose is clouded and blocked as we reside in these lower frequencies and emotions.

Tip 6

Forgive others and forgive yourself. The sooner you forgive and let go of resentment and hate, the quicker you will create space for your purpose and the opportunities the universe holds for you.

Tip 7

Remember, everything has led you up to this point, and you are exactly right where you are meant to be.

You may be wondering, what does all this talk about purpose have to do with me? My purpose is to support others to stand in their purpose, uniting in connection, trust, and love, and making the world a better place.

So, where has my purpose shown up in my life? I discovered my superpower is allowing others to shine during weekly interviews with bestselling authors, celebrities, and inspirational leaders on *The Power of the Tribe Network* TV Show. Now, after over one hundred interviews, I learned to support others to reveal their authentic self, embrace their message, and make them relatable to their audience and reach more people. I know I have achieved an amazing interview when the guest exclaims, "That was a great question no one ever asked me." In every interview, I allow them to shine.

Through my interviews, leaders get to show their authentic selves, share their stories, and become relatable. In this process, they create trust and connection for their clients, employees, and those they serve. This shifts the definition of leadership becoming more inclusive and fulfilling for all parties. The role of a great leader is no longer to lead from the top down, but instead, the triangle of power is flipped, and leaders get to listen, empower their people by removing obstacles that block their progress, and trust their teams, their abilities, and roles to contribute to a greater result. I learned this shift in leadership from the late Tony Hseish and his book *Delivering Happiness*.

Another focus of my purpose is helping entrepreneurs find their voice and let their message be heard. Like this collaborative book, I help first-time authors become international bestsellers by writing just one chapter. This also supports experienced authors in creating newly published content a chapter at a time while increasing their visibility and expanding their reach. This saves them time, money, and stress compared to writing a full book. Best of all, they gain credibility by becoming an international bestselling author. There is a synergetic power when authors collaborate. It adds layers of meaning, tied around one topic, for a sum that is greater than its parts. Also, within the project, co-authors learn the tools to build powerful networks and alliances serving them as they move forward and build their audience success.

Whether you are an entrepreneur, author, corporate executive, or emerging leader, I would love to hear from you. If you are ready to step forward, stand in your power, and have your message heard, join me and become a co-author in an upcoming anthology; your bestseller gold seal is waiting. Or establish your presence on social media with a powerful interview and connect with more of those you are seeking to reach. In all I do, I am here to make you shine.

Tip 8

Don't do it alone.

I realized that I did not need to have all the answers; I just needed to seek people who did and allow them to support me for the next leg of my journey. I allowed myself to be worthy by investing in myself, hiring mentors, and aligning with a community for collaboration, insight, and support. One of life's biggest reveals was successful people have mentors. People pay to teach them things they don't know. It sounds so simple, but this is a big hurdle for people living in a mindset of scarcity. Working with mentors is not a cost but an investment that will save you time and money. You are worth it.

Eight Tips to Help You Shine in Your Purpose:

Tip 1: Something I learned that helped me get settled after moving: when you arrive, make your bed first. There is a comfort in knowing you have one place you can lay your head when it is time to sleep and close your eyes everything else falls into place.

Tip 2: If you are feeling lonely and looking for connection and community, be willing to reach out and invite others to connect with you.

Tip 3: If you are looking to connect with other women, focus outward and serve. When you are vulnerable, open, loving, and giving, you will attract other amazing women and form your own power group. Magic will happen when you connect with others, with no expectation, and from a place of generosity. The secret is all in your state of being. Give and you will receive.

Tip 4: It is okay to try different careers and paths just keep moving. Change is not the enemy but can often lead to great discoveries. Denying your gifts and living without love and passion is the source of discontent and can lead to an unhappy life.

Tip 5: Hold space for yourself as you continue uncovering your purpose. Be kind to yourself and remember to celebrate the wins.

Tip 6: Forgive others and forgive yourself. The sooner you forgive and let go of resentment and hate, the quicker you will create space for your purpose and the opportunities the universe holds for you.

Tip 7: Remember, everything has led you up to this point, and you are exactly right where you are meant to be.

Tip 8: Don't do it alone.

As we come to the close of this chapter, I wanted to share some words of inspiration to encourage you on your journey.

Inspirational Words:

We all get to shine

What does it mean to shine?

To be comfortable in your own skin.

To love who you are and the place you hold in this world.

To influence, lead and support others, so they too can shine.

To bestow love, joy and kindness to yourself, your community, and the world around you.

To know you were placed in this world with a purpose, a mission, a legacy, only you get to carry forth.

To stand in the drift of life, stand for others who may not be able to stand or who have lost their light, and to shine on them to bring their light forward.

To embrace each day as if it were your last, for life is precious, a gift.

To sing loud and proudly, dance in the rain, and smile at all babies, humans, fur, and all creatures of the earth.

To be grateful having been placed this on this beautiful, blue marble, earth, our home.

How do you get to shine?

If I can be of any help, please reach out. I would love to hear from you.

> "When a woman loses her tribe, she loses her shine.
> But when we come together, we shine brighter."
> —Maureen Ryan Blake

Maureen Ryan Blake

Maureen Ryan Blake is a bestselling author, TV show host, and executive coach.

Her superpower is allowing others to shine during her weekly interviews with bestselling authors, celebrities, and inspirational leaders on *The Power of the Tribe Network* TV show. With over one hundred interviews, her focus is on her guest, their message, and allowing their true authentic self to shine.

Maureen Ryan Blake holds a dual master's in leadership and diplomacy from SUNY-Stony Brook. She is also a coach and graduate of HCL Transformational Leadership and is committed to leading from generosity.

Maureen's professional career started on Wall Street, working with such companies as Cantor Fitzgerald and Newscorp. She moved on to facilitate millions in federal grants that connected hundreds of businesses and thousands of students, enabling the mentoring and coaching of youth and adults to find their purpose, unlock their potential, and step into a productive and engaging life. As a serial entrepreneur, Maureen has created several successful businesses and continues to align and support fellow entrepreneurs with genuine care and gratitude.

The Power of the Tribe is a female solidarity group that serves women entrepreneurs to up-level their lives and business through the power of female friendship. Its mission is to help women find their focus and purpose and unlock their potential for greater success in business and life.

Maureen@thepowerofthetribe.com
https://thepowerofthetribe.com
619-852-4677 (private)
858-831-2220 (work)
https://www.facebook.com/groups/thepowerofthetribe
linkedin.com/in/maureen-ryan-blake
https://www.pinterest.com/thepowerofthetribenetwork/
https://www.youtube.com/channel/UC7Bxbm3OvvFbOs4dkMYHxZw
https://www.instagram.com/thepowerofthetribe/
https://twitter.com/MaureenRyanBla1

LEAN INTO THE INVISIBLE TO BE VISIBLE
BY HILARY DECESARE

Life transitions are as unstoppable as the seasons. You might even be going through one right now. However, some transitions make us feel like we can't move forward when the inevitable setback happens. Then it feels like we're stuck and don't have the control we wish we did over the situation. Have you noticed just at a time when we need momentum most, paralysis can set in? The stakes have just been raised. I've always personally believed that life transitions have a silver lining, each and every time, whether positive or negative. I would be putting this to the test with the most monumental transition of my life.

How do you feel about milestone birthdays? Do you think it means turning more than just a calendar page? Turning forty, fifty, or sixty can be great, but it's better than great when you can celebrate in style, newly remarried, having survived a cancer scare, surrounded by those you love most at a place like Silver Lake Cabin, our family getaway, full of generational memories that connect you to a continuum of eighty-five years.

Two years before the big birthday, we'd scheduled to do our annual all-hands-on-deck family cleanup of Silver Lake, but I had been feeling ill and stretched thin, and both my girls were busy that day, so the family agreed to forge ahead without the full group. Not even an hour in, an ominous rumbling came from the stove, and everyone decided it was best to call a repair person and delay the annual cleaning. So, my dad, stepmom, son, and brother packed the car back up and left. Not even fifteen minutes later, while on the main road, a screaming *whoosh* of fire trucks whizzed by. Looking back, the family saw they were taking the cabin's exit. As they hurriedly pulled up to Silver Lake, all they saw through the smoke, sirens, and commotion were flames. The family cabin had been leveled, in a matter of minutes, from a gas explosion. And although we were all devastated to lose Silver Lake, that sliding door moment of the rumble from the stove, or possibly the beloved walls warning them to leave, spared my entire family.

The new cabin was finished exactly two days before my milestone birthday weekend. We decided to christen it with a disco party theme night, costumes and all. My new husband, dad, stepmom, mother, brother, and best friends all stretched down a forty-foot-long table lit with twinkling candles. One by one, their toasts and speeches brought me back to times throughout my life, like a living album of memories.

Taking the disco-era party theme to another level, my mother sat across from me in a canary yellow lace mini dress, radiating *life* in its purest energy form. I was mesmerized by her natural way of talking from her heart, bringing her innermost self into her head and opening it to all those around her.

I was still floating on a high, not even four days after my birthday weekend, when I got the phone call that would paradoxically both change and, ultimately, clarify everything for me.

Mom's voice was different—very pragmatic, very direct, devoid of her usual warmth: "Hilary, they found thirteen lesions in my liver." One weekend after she had hiked the seven-mile trail around the lake with me, my mom found out she had cancer.

One thing about midlife is, many of us tend to think we've mastered a few things, and, with enough effort, maybe we can even control the outcome. I had witnessed many things that were *fixable*, even, in my own fortunate case, cancer. And at that moment, I was determined to add my mom's cancer to my growing "fix" list.

Having been in the high-tech corporate world for over ten years in Silicon Valley, further going on as a co-founder of my own startup companies, and the lead of an episode of ABC's *The Secret Millionaire*, I was now a twenty-year executive coach and reinvention expert, helping people launch and relaunch businesses, calling the venture The ReLaunch Co. Leaning on my twenty years of experience, our mission was to help women lean into life's transitions in order to create transformations, so they could become and have the best versions of what a successful lifestyle looked like for them, both professionally and personally. I had just founded this company when I got the call from my mom. Synchro destiny? Maybe. But I was willing to bet on anything that gave us both hope.

This impact on my own life led me to launch a podcast called "The ReLaunch Podcast," which helps listeners understand that the only way to have your life thrive on the *outside* is to focus on what is going on *inside* of you. Once you are able to do this, you'll start to become unstuck, gain momentum, and see the possibilities and opportunities awaiting when you are able to consistently show up living life, getting out of the head and into the heart. Showing up as your higher self will allow you to create the identity of your future self—aligned both on the inside *and* the outside.

Sometimes it takes another person to help us take ourselves to the next level. For me, this started with focusing with a vengeance on a new meaning and mining a new approach to help my mom survive and thrive.

I had to become one with a process that I call 3HQ™—a process that links the three key pathways from the head to the heart to the higher self, a.k.a., the 3H's. Your 3HQ™ is a merger of these essential elements that are unique to each of us, creating a whole that is greater than the sum of the parts. Basically, I came to realize this was also the foundation of the essence of my mom, the woman who had lived and instilled it within me. A woman who didn't have much longer to live showed me how to truly live.

Though IQ (Intelligence Quotient) and EQ (Emotional Quotient) have been studied continuously over the years, neither in isolation serves as an accurate prediction of success nor provides the steps to achieve it. The 3HQ™ process provides not only a basis for coping, gaining momentum, and thriving, but evolving to an elevated way of *being* and showing up authentically as your best self daily in any situation, especially difficult ones. When you understand how to access and activate your 3HQ™, your life will be changed.

Here are the ways to live and show up using The 3HQ™ in your life:

1. **The person you are today is made up of an accumulation of all your beliefs—make sure those beliefs are actually yours and are serving your higher self and the identity you wish to have.**

What if I told you that ninety to ninety-five percent of what you do in your head is automated, happening behind the scenes without you even knowing it?[2] That you couldn't get out of your head because your subconscious is pre-wired to anchor you where you are—safe, familiar, and stuck? Your beliefs are caused by repeated thoughts and emotions that have ultimately created and defined this current version of you. Your subconscious is tasked with keeping it right where it is.

You will not mentally be able to move into a new identity that can deliver the desired outcomes you are trying to manifest until you realize that you actually have control over those pre-fixed beliefs—and you then activate that control and change those beliefs. Examine and question *why* these beliefs formed. If they are not serving you, release them. How? Start by writing down all your core beliefs, then answer *why*, *when*, and *who* helped you form them. Then question if they truly come from your heart or your head. Next, decide whether they align with your higher self. Ditch the ones holding you back and your priorities in life. Once you do this, you'll be able to take your business, relationships, and goals to levels you desire and embrace that coveted level of *joie de vivre*.

2. **Our subconscious brain doesn't know the difference between positive or negative beliefs; if our thoughts dictate our reality and experiences, we must eliminate our limiting negative beliefs by changing our thoughts.**

Knowing we have roughly 6,200 thoughts a day that float through our minds, our brain defaults to its number one job, which is to rely on those pre-programmed beliefs and resulting thoughts. To put this in perspective, this is not unlike the neuro version of inheriting a million dollars and only being able to access one-tenth of your fortune.

---

2 https://www.newscientist.com/article/mg23931880-400-lifting-the-lid-on-the-unconscious/

3. To live a life from the heart to the head to the higher self, it is important to not only be a life-long learner of beliefs but understand what they are and the power they have on our lives.

My mother came by it naturally, intuitively. It was in her DNA, and I was introduced to the concept by her and the resulting gratitude and grace she inspired at the end of her life. But I didn't really grasp or understand it until I obtained a degree in psychology and other certifications. But my real learning journey was life, and it prepared me for sharing the process of how we can all fully step into our brilliant purpose.

Following my mom's cancer diagnosis, our lives consisted of doctors' appointments, new treatments, chemo, radiation, wellness and nutritionist visits, daily walks—anything she could do to get better, stay positive, and beat the cancer. And although my mom had been living from her heart to her head to her higher self almost every day of her life, I noticed an incredible shift in the way she was now really leaning in, showing up, and moving forward.

It goes against everything we are taught to start with delving inside, revealing the *invisible* first so that we can reveal and peel back the layers that are designed to protect our highest, most authentic self. Freed from our limiting beliefs, we can then step forward and that authentic self can become *visible on the outside*. The 3HQ™ secret to happiness is aligning our heart and head, revealing and showing up as the best version of our identity for the visible impact that brings us the joy and gratitude of a purposeful lifestyle.

My mom was also bringing into my life the gift of learning how to be truly grounded in my own purpose. I realized that she taught me the greatest lesson in life, going so much deeper into what I thought I knew. Built on the invisible from inside each of us, the foundation of a 3HQ™ lifestyle was more clear and powerful. The invisible, I saw, is just as important, if not more, than the visible.

Mom's cancer journey was short, only fourteen months, and on October 28, 2018, I was by her side when she passed. The veil is thin now between the invisible and the visible.

To truly step into your brilliant purpose, you must lead your life with your heart—build out your intuition and respect your emotions as you feel them. You have a choice, a great gift waiting to be opened, to learn, and live by—a 3HQ™ lifestyle aligning and uniting your heart, your head, and your higher self. Make the choice today to be the best version of who you are, and start by accessing and bringing forward your invisible, inner gifts. If you're ready to ReLaunch now and perhaps seek further clarity, join one of our available Masterclasses focused on The 3HQ™ by visiting www.therelaunchco.com. Because there's never a better time than now to step into your brilliant purpose and find your greatest happiness.

Hilary DeCesare

Hilary DeCesare is an award-winning business expert, esteemed author, host of "The Relaunch Podcast" and Radio America's "The ReLaunch." As a sought-after speaker, founder of The Relaunch Co., and creator of The Fired-Up Entrepreneur signature course, Hilary brings fresh energy to industry leaders, CEOs, and solopreneurs.

She is widely recognized for her work in neuropsychology as it relates to business and life and holds a psychology degree and several certifications from top practitioners in the field. She serves on the foundation board of Cal Poly San Luis Obispo, where she is a frequent guest lecturer on topics such as entrepreneurship and business.

As a loyal philanthropist, Hilary has been featured on ABC's hit TV series *Secret Millionaire*, where she shared the stories of people who have overcome difficult circumstances. Her insights have been seen on ABC, NBC, CBS, Fox, and mentioned in the *Huffington Post*, *Yahoo*, *Market Watch*, and others.

The culmination of her work has brought her to innovate the 3HQ framework, where Hilary empowers mid-life women to experience joy and reimagine what's possible.

hilary@therelaunchco.com
(415)562-7647
https://www.the3HQ.com/
https://www.facebook.com/TheReLaunchCo/
https://www.linkedin.com/in/hilarydecesare
https://www.instagram.com/therelaunchco/

BRILLIANT SUCCESS FOR REBELS
BY CHARLOTTE ALLEN

Is this your opportunity to make a change and follow your passions? How do you decide if it's time to change? No longer is work the same as it was for our parents or grandparents, staying at one job or company for their entire work life. Certainly, they stayed in the same industry or type of work. Through years of unhappiness or unfulfillment, they stayed. That's hard to imagine in today's age of choices. With each new generation entering the workforce, the amount of time spent at a single job has decreased, and the amount of people switching careers has increased. The global pandemic has both accelerated that movement and turned it on its head. Forbes reports more people than ever before are changing their jobs and careers.3 This movement of talent is speculated by experts to be a result of many things: remote work, better income, change in priorities, preferred locations, work/life balance, to name just a few. Employment shifts were once primarily due to seeking experiences and greater speed of advancement. Now the opportunity is to rethink our approach to work and align that with our passion and purpose.

---

3 https://www.forbes.com/sites/carolinecastrillon/2021/05/16/why-millions-of-employees-plan-to-switch-jobs-post-covid/?sh=67ef22aa11e7

During times of seismic shifts, common threads still emerge, and they often speak to the reasons. The common threads I've seen consistently across the generational shifts and the most recent pandemic shift are: 1) People want to work at something they derive meaning from. 2) They desire something different, and they are ready to take action on change. Jobs and careers are filled with busyness. Busy learning new things or busy repeating the same things. Busy taking on new assignments, increasing scope or span of control, and growing expertise base and sphere of influence. Busy can be very exciting. The pace is fast, and successes come quickly. This phase is very exciting and hopefully rewarding but also filled with challenges and obstacles to overcome. There's very little, if any, time to stop, reevaluate priorities, and take full control of this portion of our lives.

Somehow busy became a badge of honor. Too often, you must be busy to be successful. Career progression comes with increased obligations and less time for things like family and personal interests. You are also left with little time to look around, assess where you are in life, and check out other options. The lull of comfort is strong and clouds your natural instincts to seek better options. After all, once you're caught up in the spinning ride, it's difficult to step off at full speed. The unknown looms larger and larger with every passing day, month, and year. You become fearful of change partially because change is so far in the past. A distant memory of something that happened a long time ago, and you convince yourself that times are different and that change doesn't happen in your current circumstances. You've probably told yourself or gotten advice from a trusted friend or someone in a similar situation that you need to stick it out. The data tells a different story. Many of you are looking for something different. You may have reconnected with your passion or purpose or just finally had that time to reevaluate what you want from life and how you want to work. Most people still want to work for meaning and purpose.

Fear is powerful! It's a strong blocker to your thoughts and actions.

Moving forward is all about the intentionality of overcoming that fear. How do you decide when to make the shift or what to shift to?

Many people ask about my shift from a corporate employee to a solopreneur. They don't realize that was my second big shift. The first big career move I made was moving industries from healthcare to food. After working in healthcare for seven years as a respiratory therapist (with the intent to go to medical school), I loved the patients but found it hard to separate myself as I should.

The lifestyle was exciting for a while but also difficult with shift work and holidays. I intentionally made a move from healthcare to one of my other passions, food, and went back to school. After sixteen years working in the food industry, the second shift I made was the move from a corporate employee to a solopreneur. This did not come from a master plan I had created for myself. When I left corporate five years ago, I would not have been able to predict that I would become a bestselling author, creator or founder of Rebel Success for Leaders, professional speaker, and sought-after consultant. None of that was crystallized in my vision at that time, but I intentionally made a move to something different. Am I living according to my values and priorities? Absolutely, yes; that's true for both shifts. In fact, I'm sitting in the bullseye, the sweet spot, the core of where I want to be, and that was true for the prior shift as well. Values and priorities are my guide and well-aligned with my purpose.

Before both shifts, I was experiencing what most people do: a certain lull to a comfortable situation with a regular paycheck and the fear of the unknown. There was also dissatisfaction, burnout, and not being able to show up in life how I wanted to. It's true for everyone that comfort often helps us overlook the negatives. The lack of opportunity or the sacrifice is justified to be worth it. Often there's not a way to glimpse the alternate options, evaluate them and fully understand the best way to achieve them. If you are getting those nudges or feelings that things should be different, take advantage of those opportunities that come your way. Take that invitation and step out and into a very different space of opportunity. Don't let the fear of the unknown hold you back.

After reevaluating my priorities and how I wanted to be valued, stepping up to the new opportunity of creating my own business for the second shift was a no-brainer but getting there took time. Gut instinct was always something I'd followed, even when I didn't know where it was taking me. Following my gut to consider leaving was only the beginning; two big challenges remained. The first challenge was identifying the alternate options as the next steps. In the same way that the corporate world is a unique ecosystem with many common touchpoints, entrepreneurs have an almost completely separate ecosystem. How they network, the systems they use to grow their businesses, their connection to the community, and their appetite for personal growth are all unique. It was equally surprising and fascinating to me that this alternate world existed. The second challenge was the process of defining the steps and the path forward without clearly seeing the destination. For me, this part of the process seemed very similar to the discovery phase of innovation when you aren't crystal clear about what the product or service is.

What I experienced in both cases was the move from being an expert and established in one area and the discomfort with shifting in a new direction. As an established expert, you make great decisions about who to work with and what direction to take. Unfortunately, the discovery experience can be a lot like wandering in the desert with a large dose of FOMO (fear of missing out). My practice was to cycle between discovery – learn – implement – evaluate. It's the same cycle that beginning learners use all the time. Building confidence one experience at a time through testing and learning. This helped me to build on my life experiences and kept me from getting stuck in one place. The lack of confidence you have in discovery means you try lots of things and jump from expert to expert, without really finding success for a time. Changing direction feels like starting over. Not so! You have a whole set of life experiences to draw on. With a little guidance, intentional steps, and consistent action, you can emerge more successful and personally satisfied.

Here are my top, personally tested suggestions on how to wade through the process of shifting and firmly stepping into your brilliant purpose. This is not the only order possible, and it's not always linear. Rebels tend to go after things in their own order, so I'm sure you will too!

Find the Spark

A spark, by definition, is small, fleeting, easily missed, and may fizzle out quickly if not nurtured to flame. You may easily miss a spark if not on the lookout. You may also easily dismiss a spark as not relevant, important, or timely. Busy and overwhelmed can easily dismiss a spark. Some describe the spark as intuition or a nudge. As a general rule, if you've seen or heard something three times, if that nudge revisits, spend time with it. A quiet time when you can think or journal. Usually early in the morning. Try to figure out what this idea or unique passion is all about.

Discovery/Exploration

This phase is where so many people get lost. They wander around, trying everything, worried they will miss something. Many ultimately give up. The key to this phase is to be intentional and mindful. Avoid the squirrel syndrome—chasing after whatever runs past you. When innovators are in this discovery phase, they do a lot of research on what's possible and what's out there. Particularly who's having the most success in an area. This phase is also a time for experimentation. Try something out to see how it works and how it might fit you best. Look for people or organizations in a space you may be considering. It's standard practice to offer free consults or complimentary visits to gain exposure. Choose a couple of these opportunities and attend. The questions you ask yourself: 1) Can I learn something of value here, and what is that? 2) Are these the people I'd like to surround myself with? and 3) Form a duration or exit plan. None of these opportunities you identify early will last forever, so set an intention to learn, a time frame for that learning, and when you'll move on to the next one, either taking some learning with you or leaving it behind.

Seek Tension and Opposition

It's so important when you're in this phase of transformation that you find and surround yourself with supporters. Those that can provide guidance and positive energy during the process. Some call these friends, mentors, accountability partners, or coaches. If you're really fortunate, they are people who are on a similar journey, and you can all walk together. Seeking and surrounding yourself with supporters reinforces the choice you've taken or what you're creating. It's also important to include a couple of people who challenge your path and who are able to suggest new ways of thinking. These aren't the naysayers in life who hold you back but the experts who truly would have chosen differently. In the innovation communities, friction is required for the creation of something new. Successful teams are built with diverse points of view and approaches to problems. Think about your circle of experts as your team, and be sure to include those who think differently than you and can approach a problem through a different lens.

Lead Your Head Talk to Be Magnetic

Doubts are a normal part of this process, and the bigger the shift you're considering, the bigger the doubt. It's critical to quickly get control of what I call your Head Talk. It's the stuff we say to ourselves. Unfortunately, it also often doesn't have backing, support, or logic. Instead of the term mindset, which sometimes can feel like a big effort and process to manage, Head Talk is manageable. It's what we say to ourselves, and it can be scripted. You can create the language you want to hear. Making the deliberate shift from allowing it to happen to intentionally lead it for positive benefit is the change that you need. Olympian Galen Rupp asks, "Does your mind have control over you, or are you going to have control over your mind?" Once you have control of the narrative that's playing in your head and align that with your brilliant purpose, you are unstoppable!

Be Persistent/Invincible

Giving up is the easy choice. Returning to what's comfortable and known keeps us entrenched in the familiar. Why pursue the difficult path when you are probably pretty good at the easy one? Along with creating and exploring, invincibility is one of the traits that leads to Rebel Success. It's the trait where your resolve to do something gets stronger with opposition. Celebrate your discoveries, progress, and wins. Even a door closed is a celebration. It increases focus. When you are really hard on yourself, take a step back and look at your recent celebrations, even the small ones. When you celebrate more, you get more wins!

Sell/Influence

At some point, you'll need support in the form of connections or introductions. You may be pursuing a solo path and will need to be in a position to sell your product or service. Confidence plays a big role in your success. When you're confident, you tend to move forward to opportunities versus away from them. Getting really good at your abilities to sell an influence is an area to focus on. The more confident you are in your path forward, the more your influence grows. Visible confidence is a sign that others will look for in you, and when they see it, they are more willing to take a chance on you.

As you step toward your brilliant purpose, remember you are not alone; you have valuable gifts and experiences uniquely yours to bring forward. I'll say it again: only you can bring this forward! You can create a life where your work is aligned with your purpose.

If you want support on the journey, here are some resources that can help you:

In my book *Rebel Success for Leaders: Lead, Grow and Sell Fearlessly*, you'll get more specifics on how to bring your Rebel Success forward. Learn more on my website, https://rebelsuccessforleaders.com/books/, or purchase from Amazon.

From my website, you can take the Rebel Rating (https://rebelsuccessforleaders.com/rating/). It's a short assessment that will give you an understanding of where you stand on the four success characteristics and how to use them to move forward to your brilliant purpose.

Connect with me on LinkedIn (linkedin.com/in/charlotteallenfoodinnovator/) and let me know that you heard about me here. I post suggestions, blogs, and videos that you can take advantage of regularly.

I'm here cheering you on to your brilliant and purpose-filled Rebel Success!

Charlotte Allen

After years of working between or across organizations to bridge the divide that limits success, Charlotte Allen now teaches those proven strategies to individuals and organizations around the world. Using each individual's uniqueness and connecting that with the organizational purpose, Charlotte helps teams work the diversity that makes us stronger, realize the benefits of people versus process, and break the paradigm to successful change.

Charlotte works with STEM organizations and individuals in STEM fields on a broad array of topics such as leading change, organizational development, and innovation. The natural friction that comes with diverse thought is essential and requires skill to drive to success. The key principles of Rebel Success result in helping leaders free up their time to work on their vision and strategy, break the paradigm that more than 70 percent of organizational change fails by teaching people-centered change, and realizing operational flexibility from hiring a diverse team with diverse ideas and contributions.

Charlotte has over twenty years of leadership experience, including sixteen at Kraft Foods, working with iconic brands. She holds a Ph.D. from The Ohio State University and is the bestselling author of *Rebel Success for Leaders – Lead, Grow, and Sell Fearlessly*.

She is a nationally renowned keynote speaker for groups and organizations that are looking to break barriers, drive people-centered meaningful change, empower organizations, and innovate to lead the market.

Email: charlotte@rebelsuccessforleaders.com
Phone: 847-780-2084
Website: www.rebelsuccessforleaders.com
Facebook: https://www.facebook.com/rebelsuccessforleaders
LinkedIn: https://www.linkedin.com/in/charlotteallen-foodinnovator/ and https://www.linkedin.com/company/rebel-success-for-leaders
Twitter: @LeadersRebel
Instagram: @charlotteallen_rebelsuccess

THE COURAGE TO FACE YOUR PURPOSE
BY KARA GOSS

She came into our mentorship call, and her camera turned on. Her cheeks were ruby red, tears streaming down her face. I saw absolute devastation, hopelessness, frustration, and deep suffering. I gently placed my hands upon my heart, feeling deep compassion for what I was about to hold and support her through. I took a loving breath.

I asked, "What is wrong?"

Through the tears, the stumbles, and the stuttering of her words, she sobbed. "I don't know why I am here! I love helping other people." She sobbed hysterically. "When will the universe tell me what my purpose is?"

The interesting aspect about this client was she was taking all the steps along her inner journey to be well on her way to discovering her purpose. Because nothing was showing up in her business in the way she thought it should, she felt like she was a failure, had no value to offer, and wanted to quit everything. All of this angst because she wasn't getting what she saw as the status quo's definition of success looked like.

This is the struggle and the pitfall for those who seek to fulfill something within. You feel this deep inner calling inviting you to become the greatness you were designed to become. That greatness may not equal massive client bookings, likes on social media, or even a lot of money. But as you allow it to flourish, it does bring deep peace, joy, harmony, and an abundance to life that cannot ever be defined by outer, material things. Stepping into our purpose can show up in many different ways.

It is through trusting and taking the steps you are guided to take and keeping an openness to the journey you are on that your purpose finds you, not the other way around. If you think you know where you are going, you may be shocked to discover that the steps you were taking were just leading you to a totally different destination. **Having an open mind and a sense of presence with your purpose journey is crucial to discovering what you were created for.**

If you are here and reading this powerful book and have yet to discover the brilliance of your purpose, know this: it's on its way to you. Purpose for some may be an experience of the clouds parting and the angels singing, showing you precisely what you are here for, how to do it, what the outcome will be. More times than not, purpose is a discovery, a journey of daring to go after your dreams, that deep inner calling to become and create what the world told you cannot.

Your purpose comes alive when you dare to trust in your dreams, to trust in yourself, and to trust in the universe, especially when it forces you from your comfort zone, especially when you don't see a way forward. Bills, lack of money, not enough time. Perhaps, family and friends will shun you? There is always a reason not to act.

When you take the steps of your inner calling, where, at times, it makes no sense to anyone or even you, doors will open. **The universe is always conspiring to help and support you.** Time and time again, I have been guided to take steps that seemed totally illogical.

I can remember not too long ago I was instructed to close my business in my community. I was incredibly resistant; it took years to establish a spiritually based business in a deeply religious town, and it was flourishing. Clients from all backgrounds came to our events—and yes, even preachers. We had created a community of love, and it was thriving.

Then I was instructed to close everything and go online entirely. It made no sense to me at all. I had no answers for those who were saddened by my decision to close. All I could tell them was my only role is to trust that as I listen and do what I am guided to do, I will be led, even when I don't see or know the way forward. It didn't take long for me to get established online, and it didn't take long to figure out that I had just been protected when just six months later, the world was placed into massive lockdowns. Because I dared to listen to what I was feeling, to take the leap, to make a choice to have courage and push forward, I was able to help more people on a global level and have a more profound impact on others. I was also profoundly protected from losing everything that had been created through me. My community was held together, now online, and more opportunities for me to inspire others, meet more like-minded people, learn and create with others, and create a beautiful, heart-centered online community that supports all beliefs and walks of life came to be created. **When you take the steps you are guided to take, protection happens, and doors of opportunity open to supporting you.**

Getting comfortable in the unknown of your purpose journey requires deep love, trust, and courage. Every moment of your purpose is encouraging you to take these small steps toward an unknown adventure. A place where the human mind is deeply conditioned to fear when one doesn't know what is coming next and what actions we need to take. You may feel you need to know so that you feel safe. Indeed, that is an illusion. **When you don't know what is next, you are also open to the limitless possibilities that await you.** When the path you're taking seems to go silent, and no movement forward is happening. Allow the pause, get comfortable with non-action. There is no race because there is no end goal. This is an adventure without an ending. Take time for rest and resets. Remind yourself when you don't know what is happening or where you are going; miracles can easily find their way to you.

You are becoming aware of the fear mindset and choosing to shift your focus on the now moment of miraculous possibility allowing for deep peace and greater wisdom to enter your life. It also allows your heart to lead rather than your mind. **Have the courage to allow your purpose to take shape. Your purpose will often transform as you transform, and at times, it will hold more than one purpose in your life.**

There is a misconception that we are here for just one great thing, and nothing held me back more than when I believed I had to choose between dual purposes. **I had to discover that the creative force working through me**

wanted to create more than one thing. In my limited beliefs of what purpose was, I stayed stuck for two years in a place of wondering which direction I was supposed to go. Then it dawned on me: I was not picking a direction. I am here for more than one great purpose.

Purpose can express itself in various ways that seem vastly different from each other, and there are people here who will have more than one purpose. Express them all; you don't have to choose. **Be open to the fields of creation that you wish to express through your beautiful heart.** After all, you are a complex being, are you not? Why would you limit yourself to one expression? Dare to express them all!

Your purpose is a discovery of who you are, not who the world told you to be. On the path to finding your purpose or perhaps having already found the passion for what you are inspired to do, you will still have challenges. I believe challenges are designed as opportunities, for all things excellent are found in the challenges of life. Negative, not at all; the world around you and things that no longer serve you must fall away as you create new, and thus distractions arise along the path.

When we become aware of the distractions and chaos, we can sit back and smile and become calm in the storm because we know that we are indeed creating change. We are programmed to believe that life is just here taking us down again when really it is an indicator that we are growing and changing.

It is essential to find the miracles in the chaos, be the silent watcher in the storm, and not get caught up in the unraveling. If, for a moment, you do, don't worry; you can always course-correct, allow the feelings to be fully present, recenter, and refocus.

Only now can I greet this chaos with a deep smile and a bit of laughter on the inside. Knowing the changes, the challenges that greet me are indicators that opportunity is knocking on my door. I mustn't hold on to that which is falling away but allow that which is leaving to be blessed for all it has taught me in the moments I needed them—the wisdom, the growth, the discovery of my purpose.

For me, stepping into the path to discover my purpose came as an overnight spiritual awakening. My shift in consciousness occurred when awakening and spirituality were not all over social media, nor in my town. I was given inner guidance. I was taught and guided fully by spirit, and I deeply trusted in the steps I was called to take. I was a person with no understanding of spirituality, deep inner connection with source, presence, or divine love (certainly had never even heard the word *meditation*). I wasn't looking for a goal, something, or someone to become. I didn't even know at the time what was happening to me. What I did have was this deep inner peace, a presence that was guiding me, teaching me, and as I listened and acted, beautiful things began to happen. I was entirely transformed. As time went on, people I was to help began to appear. Curious, it was through being myself fully as this divine expression, showing up fully with them and as this divine love that I felt, witnessing them as fully healed, whole, perfect that they would grow and create transformations in their own lives. They saw a different way their lives could be, and it ignited within them their own deep remembrance of love, compassion, and forgiveness for themselves and another.

To me, my purpose is to love people; not love as emotional love but as the divine essence that resides within each person. It is where my bliss resides, sharing this transformational energy, words, and experiences of divine love, unity, and compassion so that others may remember they can own their divine perfection right now. As they do, they heal their unforgiveness, their suffering, their hate, self-doubt. They heal from all the things that keep a person from profoundly feeling the power of the essence which they are. I certainly never imagined or had any kind of a goal that I would be doing this as a career. That is what simply has taken shape through me staying present within my journey and allowing it to transform my life events and myself included. Simply as I chose to listen and do.

Falling into the trap that your purpose will always equal success, money, fame, or a career will steal the joy, the connection, the peace that your purpose was designed to bring you right out from under you. If it brings these things for you, excellent; you are allowed to enjoy them, but if it doesn't, it never means that you got it all wrong, that somehow you have failed, that your purpose isn't needed on the world stage. That indicates that you have more steps to take within you because you must discover that you are the purpose, your life, your expression. It has never been about another person or what you could acquire in the world. Always be willing to take the steps you are guided to take; it is how you begin to know what you are here for.

For example, I can remember a time when I thought I was to teach this one course. I still profoundly laugh when I think about it now. I put everything together, and we were off to the races. While many gained a lot of insight, so did I. I discovered that I absolutely dreaded everything about it. Yet had

I not listened to the guidance, I would not have fine-tuned what I did enjoy and what I didn't. I took the chance. I was wrong, but I was not a failure. I have many cases of this occurring as I defined what I did and did not enjoy doing. Sometimes I entirely missed the mark and were total disasters, others had profound transformational impacts, and I sincerely enjoyed the work. To me, those moments were vast and incredible successes and certainly nothing to have ever had shame about.

If you find yourself "failing," change it to redefining, fine-tuning yourself; the path of self-discovery is an ever-changing one, from moment to moment.

As a person who grew up with extreme poverty, abuse on every level, homelessness, and domestic violence, I would have never expected that stepping into the journey would have ever rewarded me with a life that brought me so much deep peace, joy, happiness, love, and harmony. Through an immense level of self-transformation, I get to share my gifts with the world. Not because of anything I have acquired or even do for a living. I live my purpose in every moment of my life. I live this way in all that I do because it fills me with so much love and beauty in the world around me. I dared to say yes to my brilliant purpose. May you be blessed with the love and the courage to do the same. I know if you are reading this, you are already doing it. I cannot wait to see where your brilliant purpose is going to take you as you dare to take the leaps of faith within your very own life. You are the miracle. I love you!

Your Purpose Journey Tips:

1. Have an open mindset.
2. Be present on the journey.
3. The universe is for you.
4. Take the steps you are guided to take (even if you don't understand why).
5. Trust and embrace the journey (it's okay to not know what is next).
6. Allow your purpose to evolve and transform as you are transformed.
7. Be open to multiple purposes.
8. Allow storms and challenges to remove what no longer serves.
9. Choose to be present, calm, and on purpose, even in the midst of a storm.
10. Dare to keep stepping into your brilliant purpose.

Kara Goss

Kara Goss experienced a radical overnight shift in her consciousness. Later she would come to understand that she was going through a spiritual awakening. Although Kara never had a physical guide, her connection to the source brought her much deep peace and transformational guidance that would assist others in having radical and beautiful life changes simply through conversations with her. As her journey unfolded, she found herself stepping more into the path of supporting others. Today, Kara's journey has led her to serve as a spiritual mentor offering teachings and transmissions to humanity based on the principles of unity, compassion, the essence of love, and the power of presence held in each now moment. Kara knows that we are in a profound evolution of human consciousness and supports teachers, coaches, and individuals to reconnect to the power of their sacred hearts—the transformational level of consciousness that heals, empowers, and connects each to a sense of deep inner peace. The connection guides them out of the conditioned responses of trauma, fear, pain, and suffering and into the transformational levels of leading a deeply empowered life held by the source of the divine within.

Email: kara@karagoss.com
Website: www.karagoss.com
Facebook: Kara Goss - Home | Facebook
YouTube: https://www.youtube.com/channel/UC5ho2uNXdvE4o-xk_cAIIkA
Instagram: https://www.instagram.com/kara_goss__/
Insight Timer: https://insighttimer.com/pub11768068

RITUALS
BY NITYA GARG, NAVELI GARG, AND MANISHA GUPTA

We are a team of mother and two daughters. While we define success differently, we all seek it without losing the freedom to be ourselves. In a world full of ideas and opportunities, such endeavors require credibility and clarity. So, we indulge in discussions where we share candidly, listen intently, and reflect collectively to understand ourselves and the world around us. Such awareness enables us to make choices that propel us toward our dual goals of success and freedom.

The topic of this chapter is rituals. Whether customary or habitual, they silently govern our lives by influencing our beliefs and shaping our personalities. We share our stories hoping that they will make you aware of the power of rituals and nudge you to intentionally choose those that propel you forward and abandon those that hold you back.

Nitya: Resurrect rituals to stay connected

Growing up, life's cards seemed to play perpetual tricks on myself and my sister. Our four-year age difference never let us coexist in the same school. Despite this, sharing a room had kept us close, giving us enough opportunities to bond. We were not just "sisters by chance" but also "friends by choice."

That was until Didi (my elder sister) moved out for college, and we grew apart.

I entered high school with renewed hopes to find someone I could call "my best friend." Never had I imagined seeing our school's emotional counselor in that role. My mom often said that nobody is a horrible person, though everyone has quirks we must be aware of, which is why I was very confident in blindly pushing my narrative. "She's overall nice," I told the counselor, "We are friends. She made a mistake." I thought bullying ended with the elementary school "don't be a bystander" workshops. Yet today, I sat in his cold yet comforting chair, listening.

I had reached my tipping point. It had been a month of being followed around, threatened to be "exposed" (silly in hindsight, scary then), and called a "fake," undeserving of affection. Then, somewhere in the aftermath, suicide rumors about me circulated.

It had become a ritual to cry after every school day. Maybe *everyone* didn't know. Maybe *everyone* wasn't telling their group, "Don't tell anyone, but I heard … about Nitya." But, perhaps, the most challenging part was accepting that somebody could hate me *this* much.

I had always considered myself a social person. As friendships became a game of hopscotch in schools, despite jumping into many friend groups, I somehow made it to the inner circle. I tried, perhaps too hard, to be there for my friends. I was the friend who stayed on call when someone couldn't sleep, asked "how are you doing" every day, genuinely cared about the response, sent pep-talk texts before tests, and made care packages to pep someone up on their bad days.

As I alternated through the friend groups, the only thing that had remained stable was my family. And today, I needed somebody, so to add to the oddities of the day, I reached out to the person seventy miles away. Didi, my older sister.

A week later, the 2020 pandemic hit. Summer swung by and brought sophomore year along with it. Didi returned but now resided in the adjacent room, despite previously sharing a room for fourteen years.

I lay lethargic on my week-old sheets through day after day of zoom school. Naps and classes seasoned time as salt and pepper season a soggy Subway sandwich. I stayed glued in my room, ignoring the world outside my bedroom walls. Occasionally, I peeped my head out for dinner and returned to my burrow to FaceTime my friends.

I was more comfortable communicating with school friends than family, a thought that sometimes became an uneasy feeling. It was fashionable for high schoolers to complain about family. I had always considered mom and sister my friends and never understood the prevalent ritual behind asking, "*Are you close to your family?*" Earlier, the answer seemed obvious: yes. I mean, I live with them, see them every day. How could I *not* be close to my family? Yet, somewhere between my Mac screen and the confining bedroom walls, I was struggling for the answer now.

After the lull came the storm—Didi and I fought. Then we talked for a long while and cried. In the rehash of a new school and weakening family bonds, I had sought refuge outside in new friends. The issue is that when we approach friendships to replace our family, we cling to every Band-Aid we find.

As we stripped away the Band-Aid and sought to connect genuinely, we have resurrected family rituals. Through family Fridays, chats, and FaceTime, we started to make intentional efforts to stay connected. I'm truly grateful I now have friends within my family and a family of friends outside—those who held me tight when I was about to fall.

Naveli: Demolish rituals that hold us back

As a little girl, I was always known to be happy. The girl who waved to all the kids, parents, grandparents, and pets, taking thirty minutes to walk a quarter-mile to elementary school. People called me a "butterfly" as I wandered in my wonderland.

This spell of happiness seems predestined to break. I was in middle school then. Walking home on a deserted trail, I stopped on a bench near a park to take a sip of water. In the far corner, a boy twice my age was taunting a girl no older than me.

"You a sexy thing. Come home with me," I heard him slur.

"No! Get away. Leave me alone." Clawing at him, she ran away.

Her strength was evident. She left me wondering why such things happen, not just to the weak but also to the strong. Wasn't the world supposed to be a happy place?

A few months later, a strung-out forty-year-old man grabbed my arm at the mall and tried pulling me into him. I was with friends, just talking. A video of a girl dancing in her room in a tank top to "Trap Queen" by Fetty Wap circulated in high school. Many spoke about the video, suggestively commenting on her body. The school administration did nothing to stop them or the circulation of the video.

These incidents kept repeating like omnipresent rituals, some customary and others forming, from newspapers describing barbaric incidents in rural areas to cars full of boys honking at a group of girls simply walking to class in universities.

My happy-go-lucky outlook shifted. Though often a bystander, I experienced trauma in others and was gravely affected by the whimsical societal constructs that give way to rude, eerie behavior. As I studied the emergence of societal constructs, the reality of the world's occasionally destructive nature sunk in. Learnings of the Stanford Rape Case of 2014, Ted Bundy, and the Nirbhaya Rape Case of 2012 further helped me understand historical suppression.

Maturing and accepting the darker side of the world, I tried to block it from interfering with my forming identity. Continuously pondering, a pivotal question formed: *Why do people do the things they do, whether good or bad?* For example, how does someone *decide* to inflict harm or do well for another? In search of an answer, I turned to study the brain, specifically decision-making. Recognizing intrinsic motivations (why one does something) can help us understand the extrinsic frameworks that govern us (the societal constructs we fit ourselves into).

Flashbacks to the park girl led me to a women studies class. Intrigued by the duality of vulnerability and femininity in the patriarchy, I wondered how learned societal behaviors had shaped us. Though a rude awakening, I found comfort in cognizing the stigma surrounding women empowerment. Not only do adverse events directly correlate to the brain's health, even the aftermath of divulging the trauma can halter our thoughts from progressing. For instance, rape culture and victim-blaming are known to silence the survivors, a conscious societal decision.

Through numerous life stories and neuroscience classes, I learned how lasting scars from repressive rituals preclude us from living a wholesome life. Yet, little to no research approaches the intersection of women-specific hardships and oppression with brain development and decision-making skills.

I aim to understand, devalue, and break societal stigmas around trauma through a scientific lens. We may not be able to eliminate all trauma. But, armed with such knowledge, we can *demolish the rituals prohibiting generations from staying blissfully happy and avoid forcing them toward distressful awareness* as they enter adulthood. Somewhere there is also my path back to the ever-happy girl I was born to be.

Manisha: Create rituals that make us feel wholesome

Every night, I would hold her hand and ask, "Are you at peace?" Every night, she would extend the other hand, a cue to help her get up. We would climb the stairs, hug each other good night, and move into our respective rooms to sleep.

A week had passed. I was to fly back the next day. The sun was finally out, filling the family room with bright rays pouring in from the life-size window.

We had been exchanging childhood memories all afternoon. Shalu Didi, my husband's cousin, fondly remembered and vividly elaborated on her childhood days. An army of maids at her disposal—massaging her hair, adorning her hands with henna. She referred to her mother as "my soulmate" as she narrated the story of the two characters flawlessly executing their covert mission to have Didi participate in a beauty pageant. Unfortunately busted by newspaper headlines declaring Shalu Didi as Ms. Ajmer. Her dramatics were in full swing as she animated how they had pleaded guilty and rolled out in laughter the moment they had the room. She was still beautiful. Still lively.

Shalu Didi had wanted to stay in her hometown. However, grandiose dreams of her soul-mate mother saw her marrying into a reputed family and moving to the USA. Rituals transitioned the princess into a perfect cook, a perfect maid, a perfectly silent wife, and a regular pay stub and insurance provider.

She had wanted kids. "I love dressing up and dressing girls up," she had chuckled, lying on that couch staring at the wieldy bamboo plant stationed on the right edge of the partition wall.

My eyes, glued on the tea pan, glanced at her. The bamboo and Didi aligned in one straight line; their strength concealed behind their untimely wrinkles.

I watered the plant. We drank the tea in silence. Then, passing the cup back, in the usual "I don't want to disturb anyone" manner, Didi whispered that her eyes were burning. I dipped two cotton balls in freshly squeezed cucumber juice and signaled her to lay her head on my lap. A few minutes later, she slept, her face calm as the cucumber juice relaxed her eyes, and I pressed her head. I was meditating in the faint rhythms of her heartbeat when she proclaimed, "Today, I feel wholesome."

"Why just today?" My eyes quizzed her. "Why not every day?" Remembering the mark their family had made in Ajmer, I urged, "Would you like me to record your stories? Narrate. I will write."

Her eyes twinkled; she nodded, then quickly corrected, "He (her husband) may not approve." She was right.

We used to call Shalu Didi's mom "Pyaari Maa," who indeed lived up to that name lovingly taking care of everything for everyone. Maybe so much that Didi never learned self-care.

All the talking had visibly tired her. She wanted to retire to bed early. So, I ritually held her hand and repeated yet again, "Are you at peace?"

I realized that my eyes had given away more than I had wanted as she spelled out loud, "In case I don't wake up?" and indulged, "Yes, I am at peace. I forgive everyone."

Our hug was firm and long that night. Then, as we disentangled from each other, years of restless hopes and fears transferred from one body to another, making her stories an integral part of my being. I could not sleep that night, no more sure if I was right in expecting her to be at peace.

A few days later, she texted, "I am in the hospital. At peace," and succumbed to cancer, a disease known to thrive under chronic stress, leaving me to wonder if things might have been different if we had created rituals that made her feel wholesome every day.

The Power of Rituals

Society flourishes when we create wholesome people. We believe it's the freedom to be ourselves that makes us feel wholesome. Becoming a wholesome being is a process of self-discovery and growth—a series of choices and rituals that leave ensuing marks, define our beliefs, and shape our personalities. We endeavor to make people conscious about creating and continuing traditions that help us grow while abolishing those that hold us back.

Intentionality to bring forward the rituals that respect and uplift each other is vital for us to step into our brilliant purpose. So, we invite you to indulge in conversations that bring clarity and build credibility. When we talk, let's really talk.

Tips for the Connection Rituals:

1. Schedule a regular time to connect.
2. Observe and nurture habits that positively impact your state of mind.
3. Be intentional about creating and continuing practices that help us grow while abandoning those that hold us back.
4. Value perspectives over judgment.
5. When we talk, let's share candidly and listen intently.

Nitya Garg, Naveli Garg, and Manisha Gupta

We are a team of mother and two daughters who bond over projects and clean slate conversations. Our journey started with CharityDress, which has clothed over one thousand individuals across the world. We launched NaviNiti to stir tough conversations using arts and stories. We write to share stories that rekindle close ties with families, friends, and ourselves.

Nitya Garg is a high schooler who strives to bring attention to complex topics shaping her generation. She is an active member of school leadership, a varsity debater, a national level dancer, singer, and painter.

Naveli Garg is an undergraduate studying neurobiology, women studies, and dance at UC Davis. She aspires to research the brain and deepen our collective understanding of human behaviors.

Manisha Gupta (mother) is a technologist by trade and psychologist by hobby. Her expertise at the intersection of product and customer success has helped grow companies like LinkedIn, eBay, and CafePress. She leads Oracle's product charter for people and business analytics.

Email: team@naviniti.com
Phone: 408 307 0684
Website - www.naviniti.com (primary)
Facebook: https://www.facebook.com/NaviNiti.Motion
LinkedIn: https://www.linkedin.com/company/naviniti
YouTube: https://www.youtube.com/c/naviniti

SECTION 3:

Step Forward and Shine!

SHINE IN YOUR BRILLIANCE!
BY REBECCA HALL GRUYTER

Lately, I have been thinking about hearts, about how we are all connected through a common heartbeat, energy, that—when we open ourselves up to that magical collective heartbeat—lifts us up and brings us closer to our brilliant purpose.

Our bodies are made up of energy, often known as the human energy field. Every thought, emotion, belief, atom, molecule, cell, tissue, and body system is composed of energy. Energy emits a vibration and, whether we know it or not, we all are sending out vibrations. We have different frequencies, different messages, different things that are getting amplified out with each beat of our hearts.

This is a powerful thing to know when we think about our purpose. What are we being called to bring forward? **Ask yourself:**

What are you echoing out?

What are you choosing to share out into the world, heartbeat by heartbeat?

The beauty is that we have the choice to bring our unique vibration forward. It's not something outside of us; it's something within us.

Are you familiar with crystals? Crystals are a special kind of "liquid rock" formed when liquids cool and harden over time. As they cool, the liquid molecules fit together in a repeating pattern to form all sorts of unique shapes, sizes, and textures.4 We're most familiar with the gems that are crystalline-like opals, emeralds, and rubies. There are many more types of crystals, from amethyst to citrine, selenite to quartz, all with their own structures, colors, shapes, clarity, and vibrations.

Crystals have different kinds of frequencies that have been measured by geologists. They all vibrate a little bit differently.5 I've become fascinated with crystals, studying what their frequencies mean, how they interact, and how they connect. I loved to inspect and reflect on my crystals and began to notice how some of them have fractures, sometimes an internal crack, cloudiness, a chip, or a break that formed at some point along a weak area of its structure.

When these chips, cracks, and breaks made me sad, I decided to learn more about them. I think about the millions of years it has taken for these beautiful crystals to come to be, and I begin to see the story of their "life's" journey. I saw their fractures and breaks as wounds, and sometimes they have shattered under the force of immense pressure. Those pieces then become another form and shape, and the crystal lives on, growing and developing. As they change size, shape, and structure because of fractures or chips, they then reflect light and energy differently.

Then I learned that there is actually a term for this: ***warrior crystals.*** A warrior crystal is one that has been damaged at some point during its development by a fracture, crack, or shattering. But is it actually "damaged"? When a crystal breaks into pieces, each piece changes vibration or frequency.6 It now has more surfaces that face the light, reflecting light more powerfully and in more directions. It can serve in more places and in more ways. The power of the pieces is more amplified than ever before. So, perhaps, the crystal can now serve in more ways and more powerfully because of the chip, wound, or fracture. I believe the same is true for us, that because of our wounds, scars, and cracks, we are able to reflect more light and serve more powerfully.

---

4 https://www.britannica.com/science/crystal
5 https://www.sciencedaily.com/releases/2018/05/180521154243.htm
6 https://www.sedonamedium.com/amp/the-empathic-warrior-crystal

Lessons from the Warrior Crystal

How amazing it is to be able to look at our own wounds and scars as challenges we have faced that have dramatically shaped us!

Just as the warrior crystal has experienced enormous pressure, changes, and trauma, so have we. The crystal is just as beautiful (maybe more so) in its perfect imperfections. The crystal is experienced and seasoned and shows us its beauty and strength through it all.

I believe each of us has gone through times of great pressures and major shifts around us. We have had wounds and chips. We have had losses. If we look back over the last few years, there is a lot that the entire world has gone through. Let's make sure we are looking at these experiences through the lens of the warrior crystal: We are here; we have been shifted in a new way. We have more facets that are being revealed. We are discovering new strengths and new opportunities to serve.

Are You a Warrior Crystal?

As we think about those pressures and wounds, we realize they have equipped us to serve at a higher level, to reflect out in a bigger way to reach more people. We can bring our brilliant purpose to light even more powerfully because of the things we have faced and how we have triumphed over them.

Like the crystals, the more we experience and the more we learn and grow from that experience, the greater the vibration we echo out into the world. We have an opportunity to serve in all different places and in all of these new shapes and forms that are being created within us.

What might it look like to be a warrior crystal?

Moving to a new location. Lately, it feels to me like so many people I know are moving to new locations. Your new opportunity might be moving away or changing your current environment in some way that better supports you and your purpose. Change can bring feelings of loss: When I hear of a friend moving away, I feel the loss for a time and then realize they are taking exciting new forms of serving in another place and doing the work they are called to do.

Since our energy and vibrations are boundless, we are still connected. Now they are bringing their gifts and energy to another part of the world, further living out their purpose.

Expanding your business. The pressures and challenges of the last few years seem to have sparked new energy in people to make changes they had been thinking about (and postponing) for a while. Use the lessons of the warrior crystal to remind yourself that you also have expanded in powerful ways. Allow this knowledge to carry you forward to embrace those changes, take risks, and make the bold decisions that will bring you closer to your brilliant purpose.

Being willing to learn. Acknowledging our own warrior wounds can have our energy shifting into self-criticism, negativity, or resistance. It's important to catch that and say, *Wow. What an opportunity is in front of me! Now that I know this new part of me, let me find out what that might be!* In those moments, fear and resistance often arise as well and can show up as stubbornness. Don't let that happen; instead, open yourself up and be willing to learn. That's when you discover another area you can expand and grow in. Be willing to let the journey remove what no longer serves so that your gifts, brilliance, and light can shine more fully in the world. This allows you to shine brilliantly in your mission and purpose.

Look for and Listen to the Gems

The next time you see a crystal that has a chip or a gem that looks "imperfect," I want you to see it as a special reminder to you that you are wonderfully made. You are continually changing your shape and your design and how you serve. Each change is an opportunity for new parts of you to be revealed that can be shared out to impact the world.

Be on the lookout for an area where you can grow. From my discovery journey with warrior crystals, I was reminded that I could grow in the area of asking for support from others. I don't have to figure it out all on my own. I've made a new commitment to receiving what it is that I need, as well as what I am willing to receive. I feel I am now better equipped to make that choice.

Warrior crystals have also reminded me about connections, how valuable and beautiful they are when we accomplish things together! I want to have seasoned experts, friends, colleagues, and family around me. They have weathered storms and allowed the storms and challenges in life to transform and fine-tune how they show up in the world. They shine their purpose powerfully, purposefully, and clearly out into the world. I want to have these "warrior crystals" by my side, and I, too, want to want to walk as a warrior crystal.

What is an area where you can grow, using your new warrior-crystal strengths?

Once you feel the idea of your different facets and brilliance, your choices in storms and challenges will come into clearer focus. You get to be surprised by how your purpose and support will unfold in unexpected ways! You get to be supported in bringing your message and your impact forward, heartbeat by heartbeat. Be willing to say yes as you feel the call of your purpose and honor the chips/wounds/scars/scratches/breaks in yourself and others. Look for the beauty and light that is now being able to reflect out and shine into the world because of these "wounds/imperfections." In fact, I believe we are perfect in our imperfections and can serve more powerfully and deeply because of them. They allow light to shine through the cracks.

Some Questions for Reflection

What are you leaving behind?

What are you building toward?

Are you moving in that direction on purpose and with purpose?

What are you sharing and purposefully shining out into the world?

These are powerful questions. Take a moment, right now, to stop and integrate. Find a quiet place to sit. Take a few slow, deep breaths to settle yourself. Then, breathe in what would serve you to release what is no longer up to date. Then release that and take another cleansing breath. Now breathe in taking in what is, what you want to bring forward because you want to have the impact you are called to have.

Next, bring in your community—all the common heartbeats of the authors in this book (including mine!)—and others whose connection and energy you love to have around you. Breath in these vibrations and heartbeats and allow your heart to beat with ours in unison.

We all want you to shine brilliantly on all facets, the places and planes that you have, and those that are being created. You matter, your voice matters, you are needed. Lean in to share the amazing gift of *yourself*.

The Magic of the Collective Heartbeat

I hope that you were able to feel the energy of support from those you called in just now. Feel free to repeat this little practice as often as you like, when you want to be lifted up by your community and reminded of your warrior crystal vibration.

When we have a group of people who have this common heartbeat, there's something magical that gets created beyond what any of us could create alone. When we come together, synergistically combining our gifts and our talents and our wisdom, magic happens!

As you step into your brilliant purpose, I also hope that you will take the lessons of the warrior crystal with you to work into your life on each step that will bring forth all that you are called to bring. Please remember to take with you on this journey grace, kindness for yourself, and the joy of getting to know yourself on a deeper level.

When you are faced with something that creates a chip or fracture, remember that you have actually changed your energy and vibration. You will have new facets to reflect the light, reflecting your brilliance in more directions and shining more powerfully than ever before. May you stand as the warrior crystal you are and SHINE!

Rebecca Hall Gruyter

Rebecca Hall Gruyter is a global influencer, number one international bestselling and award-winning author, compiler, an in-demand publisher, popular radio show host (on over ten networks), and an empowerment leader. She has built multiple platforms to help experts reach more people. These platforms include radio, TV, books, magazines, the Speaker Talent Search, and live events, creating a powerful promotional reach of over ten million!

Rebecca is the CEO of RHG Media Productions, which has helped over eight hundred authors become bestsellers! She has personally contributed to over thirty-five published books, multiple magazines and has been quoted in major media, the *Huffington Post*, ABC, CBS, NBC, Fox, and Thrive Global. She has been recognized as one of the top ten working women in America by AWWIN, Inc., and now helps experts get quoted in major media too.

She wants you to have impact! Be seen, heard, and SHINE!

http://www.YourPurposeDrivenPractice.com
http://www.RHGTVNetwork.com
http://www.SpeakerTalentSearch.com
Rebecca@YourPurposeDrivenPractice.com
Radio Show: www.EmpoweringWomenTransformingLives
Podcast Show: https://www.voiceamerica.com/show/3984/the-authors-journey
Facebook: www.facebook.com/rhallgruyter
Facebook: www.facebook.com/pages/Rebecca-Hall-Gruyter/442052769207010
LinkedIn: www.linkedin.com/pub/rebecca-hall-gruyter/9/266/280
Twitter: www.twitter.com/Rebeccahgruyter
Instagram: RHGTVNetwork
Pinterest: www.pinterest.com/RebeccaHallGruyter

LET FORGIVENESS COLOR YOUR WORLD
BY MACKENZIE NELSON

Forty years ago, a man met a woman for their third date at a restaurant. He noticed her demeanor was different than the previous dates: she seemed anxious, worried, and preoccupied. The smile that made his heart flutter was gone, and he excused himself to go to the restroom to think about what might be troubling her. With a supernatural certainty and confidence, he headed back to the table, determined to ask her a very personal question. In fact, the very insinuation could have easily offended my mother and ended not only their evening but also their relationship.

"Are you pregnant?" he boldly asked, seemingly out of the blue: both of them knowing they had not yet been intimate together.

Taken aback, she replied in shock, "Yes, yes I am," knowing full well that her confirmation disclosed intimacy with another man. Over the course of the next few weeks, they discussed their future together, and Paul decided that he wanted to marry her, and knowing the baby wasn't his, he simultaneously said yes to be my father too. Following their conversations, they were married on February 7, 1981, and later that year, in September, I was born.

At age six, my mother sat me down at our kitchen table and said, "Paul is not your real father. Your father was a very bad man who did not want me to have you." My world and my face immediately drained of color. I remember glancing quickly over to the man I'd called "Dad," who was also seated at the table for the big announcement. He had remained silent while she spoke, but I screamed, "You're not my *real* father!" and I ran away from the table to go cry in my room.

I wanted answers. I needed to know who he was, where he was, and why didn't he want me? Starting at age six and throughout my teen years and early adult life, I never stopped seeking answers from my mother. No matter how I asked, simply bringing up the topic immediately triggered and angered my mother. "He was in the mafia, MacKenzie. He killed people. He was an awful, awful man." Her words cut into me like a thousand knives. "You can never find him, MacKenzie. If you do, he may kill you, and if he doesn't kill you, he will certainly kill me." I was terrified of my own biology. Adding to my confusion, there were times when she would bring him up in seemingly casual conversations while never addressing my questions directly, and when this occurred, it would either be some new information or a different version of a story I thought I already knew.

Thoughts of him swirled inside my head like little tornados destroying any remaining remnants of my vibrant, happy childhood. It was gone. In exchange, I was tormented by his absence and left to my own devices to figure out what it all meant. I was drowning and consumed with emotions and questions I did not know how to handle or process, and my mother was my only resource, the only connection I had to my biological father. I needed her more than ever, but instead, she pulled away, thinking the issue must be my strong will, so she went about breaking me with her own version of tough love. Any question or comment I had about him was interpreted by my mother as an act of defiance, and I was further punished verbally and/or physically, but the worst was the isolation. She'd send me off to my room for hours at a time. Alone. Confused. Sad. Mad. Silenced. This continued for years.

Eventually, all of her punishments, all of the public and private humiliation culminated, and as time went on, I no longer knew any of the beautiful things that used to give my life joy and vibrancy. I forgot what color carefree was, and I could no longer remember which one represented happiness, and my favorite ones, silliness and fun, had been long lost. Her vision was limited by pain and hurt, and she lived in black and white, not colored with the infinite possibilities and perspective that healing could bring. She blocked the color from entering her world, and as a result, she stole it from mine. She methodically drained, strained, and removed every single shroud of color from my life by training me to live in the black and white with her: a lonely, burdened place where we blame other people for our pain, remain victims, and as a result, victimize others in the process.

By the time I was ready to give birth to my son, Lincoln, in 2011, I was trapped, confined. I was living and breathing in her words and in the story she had written for me. Every harsh word she spoke over me throughout my childhood manifested and formed pages and pages of my identity and defined my relationships with others. My mother had concocted a colorless world full of ever-changing rules and limitations, and I had to stay bound within those pages or risk losing her and my family forever.

I gained seventy pounds while pregnant with Lincoln, and by the time he was almost three years old, I weighed three hundred pounds. Why was I over-eating to this extent? When I could barely buckle my seat belt on a plane, I knew I needed to take action. Around the same time, I heard about a forgiveness exercise where you picture an empty jail cell in a dark room. Next, you ask God, "Is there anyone I need to forgive?" And then you picture the jail cell again and see if anyone populates, so out of curiosity, I tried. I closed my eyes and envisioned the cold, dark jail cell. To my great surprise, there was my biological father standing in the cell. How long had I kept him in there? I took the key out of my pocket, put it in the lock, and felt the weight of the iron door as I pulled it open. His eyes met mine, we hugged, and I released him from the cell and watched him walk out of that room into a beautiful, sunny day. Tears flowed from my eyes without explanation for the next three days, but I knew God was healing me.

After I forgave him, I started to lose weight. I had felt buried beneath the extra pounds, and I felt hopeless about losing them. Forgiving my biological father for abandoning me changed everything. God renewed my hope and revived my spirit, and what once seemed insurmountable now seemed possible. It's been a work in progress, but six years and another baby later, I'm currently at seventy-five pounds lost overall and still actively working at being the healthiest version of myself physically, emotionally, mentally, and spiritually.

Knowing God and following Him became my purpose instead of making my mother happy. I made a choice and decided to fully pursue His will and path for my life, and He led me to get on Ancestry.com. I discovered my biological father died years ago, and I mourned the possibility of ever meeting him in this life. No cards. No flowers. No condolences. No mention of me in his obituary. I forgave him again and again, and some days, I still have to: forgiveness isn't a one-time thing. With news of his death, I was finally set free from the constant wondering. I realized I spent my childhood focused on the wrong man entirely. My dad, Paul, had chosen me before I chose him, and for the first time, I was able to openly accept the love he had freely offered all along. We have never been closer.

The journey of discovery, truth, forgiveness, and healing has damaged relationships with my mother, sister, grandmother, brother, and other family members. Coming to a place where I could see myself as more than the man my mother said defined my character has presented challenges and placed strains on these relationships. I continue to reach out and offer opportunities to reconnect and have open, honest conversations to put us on the path to healing. Each person has the unique ability to see and experience the world through their own eyes, and we should celebrate different perspectives instead of rejecting them because they are different from our own.

God has led me here, fully unleashing and downloading a new perspective brimming with hope, radiance, and vibrant color. This life of full color has been there all along: that plush, rich, redeeming story, but my eyes had been set and trained to filter all the color out for so long. I would have missed the beauty of my scars if I didn't trust God and where He was leading me. Free from the rigid rules of a black-and-white lifestyle, a new chapter and a fresh start began to come into focus. Suddenly, as if he were a living, breathing prism dispersing beams of light, there he was: my dad, Paul. He chose me the day he decided to marry my mother full-well, knowing I was not his biological child. Why wasn't *that* the story that was shared and celebrated around my home? My dad Paul, the *hero*! Because I truly believe my mother couldn't see it and that's why she never told me about that day in the restaurant. She could only see the pain and hurt, so that's the heartbreaking, terrifying story she passed down to me, my siblings, and friends and family.

Although we are not in communication, I love my mother more now than ever. Without her actions, I would not be who I am today. The tremendous trauma and pain I experienced in my childhood and still work through today have molded me into the warrior I am now. God has emboldened me to step up and share my story through my perspective: something I've never had the ability to do without feeling shame or allowing the fear about what other people might think to stop me.

Mom, if you're reading this, I forgive you. I love you. I believe there is the possibility for a new beginning for us, too. Regardless of what happens between us in the future, this is the story I will choose to pass down to my children now. Your grandchildren. One of healing. One of restoration. One where hope is never lost. One where I honor Paul and the choice he made to be my father.

Is there someone you might be struggling to forgive today as you read this? I challenge you to take a moment, close your eyes, and ask God. Picture the jail cell and see if there is anyone there to unlock the door, forgive and release. It may just be the beginning of your transition from a life lived in hurt with a wounded, limited perspective to unleashing God's healing and bringing fresh lenses and a restored, new perspective that changes everything. This empowering journey has led me to write my full story in a book called *My Father's Feathers* to be released in 2022. You can get on my list for updates about its release by going to www.mackenziekaynelson.com.

Do you have more questions about forgiveness or anything I wrote about today, or are you struggling to see your circumstances with a fresh perspective? Are you looking for someone to pray with you and for you as you walk out difficulties with a lack of support from others? I know from my own experience that when the pain cuts so deep, it is hard enough to think about it, let alone speak about it to someone else, but I've found hope and healing on the other side of fear, and I believe I can help you, too. Please contact me. I promise I'll listen, judgment-free. I'm here to lift you up, pray for you, and hold space for you.

MacKenzie Nelson

MacKenzie Nelson is a new author who knows her story of faith and freedom can help you on your own journey. She is stepping out and sharing her personal story in these difficult times to offer you encouragement, hope, and the ability to connect with her personally.

MacKenzie Nelson lives in central Illinois with her husband, Brett, and two small children. She earned a bachelor's degree in business administration from Midstate College in 2009 and is a former high school all-state basketball player. During her professional career, she worked for the American Red Cross advocating for blood donation. However, it's her perseverance, faith, and triumph over hard personal circumstances she continues to navigate that she will utilize to help you overcome your challenges. By helping to shift your perspective, you will be enabled to see your circumstances with brand-new lenses and claim victory over them. For further updates about her upcoming solo book and to get in touch with MacKenzie Nelson, visit mackenziekaynelson.com.

Email: mackenziekaynelson@gmail.com
Website: https://www.mackenziekaynelson.com https://www.myfathersfeathers.com
Facebook: https://www.facebook.com/mackenzie.nelson.545
LinkedIn: https://linkedin.com/in/mackenzie-nelson-04a5b422
Twitter: @NelsonKenz

THE DECIDED HEART EFFECT
BY SONJA MONTIEL AND HILARY BILBREY

Stepping into your brilliant purpose sounds so joyous, and it is, but it is not a passive process. Going from a life by default to a life of your brilliant design starts when we courageously choose to take that first step with a decided heart. Your decision will set into motion a whole wave of positive change in your life and in the lives of those around you. We call this The Decided Heart (DH) Effect.

To achieve a decided heart effect, there are three stages people pass through Self-Discovery, Trust Building, and Sense of Belonging. Each of these stages builds on the next and is constantly being reaffirmed. Once you embrace each stage, you will find that you won't just be stepping into your brilliant purpose; you will be illuminating the whole path.

Self-Discovery

Most humans don't actively seek self-discovery until there is a catalyst that gives them the opportunity. Sometimes the opportunity is a class, a book, an interesting person who shifts our thoughts. More often, we find ourselves in the middle of what author Bruce Feiler calls a "lifequake," a pile-up of disruptors that leaves us questioning who we are.

Coauthor Hilary Bilbrey's lifequake came on April 6, 2003, on the heels of planning her own funeral after an overzealous doctor predicted she would die giving birth to her second son. Luckily, she did not die, but the stress caused her to go into premature labor, and so the family spent a week in the hospital until their baby was ready to come home. Hilary settled back into their family's brand-new house and was ready for the "perfect" life to begin. She thought the trauma was over, but it was just beginning.

The morning of April 6, Hilary left the house for a short walk with her friend. Her husband, eighteen-month-old son, and preemie were home alone. In a split second, while her husband was changing the preemie, the eighteen-month-old managed to get into the master bath and turn on the hot water, quickly suffering severe third-degree burns. Hilary and her husband believed their house was safe. They followed all the procedures to baby-proof their home. They trusted that the plumbing company had set the "kid-safe" temperature gauge correctly. They thought they were doing all the right things, but in an instant, everything changed.

Her toddler was transferred through three different hospitals on his way to the burn center over two hours away. His screams of pain during the ambulance ride will haunt her forever. When they arrived at the burn center, his vitals crashed. The nightmare was far from over.

The next month was filled with skin grafts, debridement, investigations, and a complete shattering of Hilary's identity. She had one job as a mom—to keep her kid safe—and she had failed. Hilary couldn't help thinking that if she wasn't a good mom, who was she?

Now, there is much more to the story. Most importantly, not only did Hilary's son recover faster than doctors predicted, but he also went on to play high school varsity basketball, despite severe foot scarring and is now a thoughtful and caring young adult. For her son, his identity was not defined by his injury.

However, a year after the accident, Hilary lived in darkness, self-doubt, and anxiety. She felt like a phony—putting on a smile for the public, but inside she was emotionally beating herself up for her failure. Worse, she just didn't know who she was supposed to be anymore. The only thing that was truly going right was her one friend who always left her feeling stronger, more joyful, more connected.

It was this friend who introduced her to a whole new language of virtues (The Virtues Project™). Her friend started recognizing her for her ability to care, her excellence, the love that Hilary consistently showed up with every day and to everyone. Hilary started to question, "What if being the 'perfect mom' was never really what my identity was supposed to be?"

She then started to do the work of unpacking what she thought her identity relied on. She was not the roles she played. What defined her identity, no matter the experience she faced, were the virtues she always had with her. For her, it was integrity, compassion, and excellence. Once Hilary anchored her identity to her virtues, she began to feel like she could live again.

Our identities are how we decide to show up. If we connect to our true selves, discover the virtues that are within our hearts, and decide to consistently bring those virtues to the world, no matter the lifequake, we know who we are. We cannot be shaken.

Nearly two decades later, after three kids, countless moves, hundreds of clients, and many more lifequakes, Hilary has never lost sight of who she is. April 6, 2003 was one of the most terrifying days of her life, but the gift from pain was this journey to self-discovery.

To step into your brilliant purpose, first, take a moment and anchor to the virtues in your heart. How have you shown up in the world? How is that different from or consistent with how you want to show up in the world? Is it with joy, confidence, generosity? Perhaps it's with patience, courage, flexibility? Claim these virtues as your identity. Live them consistently in all walks of your life. When you can align who you are at home with who you are at work and who you are with friends, then you are living with a decided heart.

Complete the mantra below with a word that describes how you want to show up in all walks of your life.

Decide. Say it. Repeat it. Live it.

The DH Effect Self Discovery Mantra:
I show up with _____.

Trust Building

Owning who you are and how you show up is always the first step of truly walking in your brilliance. When you are clear about who you are and the virtues you anchor to, it brings out confidence and self-trust that helps you to engage with the world on a whole different level. Until you trust yourself, it is very difficult (if not impossible) to trust others, and without building trusting relationships, we cannot hope to have a larger positive impact on the world. Trust is where the magic happens. One light can brighten a small area, but a group of luminaries can illuminate a whole path.

"Will you have lunch with me?"

The very concept of The DH Effect was born out of Sonja and Hilary building a high trust relationship. In March 2020, right before the world shut down for the 2020 pandemic, Hilary was presenting on self-discovery to a group of micro-entrepreneurs. Sonja was in the audience. Watching Hilary passionately speak about the decisions we each can make about our innate virtues spoke to Sonja's heart. To this day, she likes to claim that she asked Hilary out for their first date. It was a lunch that instantly bonded them together because they each decided to show up with their virtues and the intention to build a trusting relationship. Within weeks, they launched The DH Effect with a mission to help others *decide* to thrive.

That's where trust starts—by finding shared interests. That only happens when we are willing to be vulnerable, open, and curious. We must decide to hold space for other people's stories so we can truly see them and be seen in return. The magic happens when we are not distracted by what is seen on the outside but instead focus on who we are at the heart level. When our goal of interacting with others is to reach this type of connection, we are able to drop defensiveness, doubt, and competitiveness and get straight to forming meaningful relationships that lift us.

As we said earlier, one candle alone doesn't give off as much light as when you start adding other candles. For Sonja and Hilary, their goal is to celebrate each other's strengths, support each other's challenges, and most importantly, consistently prove themselves trustworthy by delivering on promises. Each of them makes an intentional decision to show up in these ways every day for each other. For example, Sonja is a master at creating systems. Hilary thrives when she is allowed to strategize. Sonja trusts Hilary to create a big picture. Hilary trusts Sonja to help ground it in actionable steps. Neither one is more important. They are both necessary to the process.

In this same way, when we think of the relationships in our lives, are we showing up first with a true intent to listen and be curious about the other person? Are we looking for opportunities to find shared values and interests? Are we willing to step back and let someone else shine in their strength, trusting that you will also get the opportunity to step into your own brilliance? Do you trust yourself enough to be confident in what you bring to the relationship?

We become better and shine brighter when we build high trust relationships in our lives. If trusting yourself and others is uncomfortable for you, start to shift your mindset with the second mantra below. If you discover that you are doubting yourself or feel afraid to connect with others, repeat this mantra.

Decide. Say it. Repeat it. Live it.

The DH Effect Trust Building Mantra:
As I trust myself, I extend healthy trust to others.

Belonging

Look up "success and belonging" in any search engine, and you will find more research than you will ever be able to get through. You will find that one of the biggest indicators of success is a sense of belonging. How do we nurture that in ourselves? How do we nurture it in our relationships?

Sonja has a beautiful illustration from her childhood of how we can create belonging, even in the most difficult of situations.

"Girls."

"Yes, Papa?"

"Mom and I have exciting news to share with you…"

Sonja and her twin sister were seven at the time. Their mother and father were at the kitchen table, sitting next to each other. They were holding hands. You could see it in the girls' squinting eyes and clinched fists that the anticipation was too much to wait for.

"You will be living in two houses!"

They jumped with glee. Yup, they were celebrating their parents' divorce, although their parents never used that word. The girls didn't know it was a bad thing, and honestly, it wasn't because their parents decided to change the context of divorce and create something positive for the entire family. Sonja and her sister's sense of belonging to two adults who loved them unconditionally was all that mattered.

As they helped their mother pack up her belongings and move out of their home, they witnessed their parents supporting each other. Their father was lifting the heavy furniture and organizing the back of a pickup truck carefully. When their mother and father would pass each other on the sidewalk, Sonja and her sister witnessed them exchanging smiles. To them, the context of the divorce meant nothing more than getting two homes.

To them, the most important singular thing remained in their lives—family, a place (in this case, places) where they were trusted and could be trusted. This was their anchor to belonging. It was an experience that has helped Sonja make decisions over and over again throughout her lifetime, avoiding quick reactions to changes in context, and instead, embracing the questions that brought about the power of belonging:

"Who are my people in this context?"

"What is my contribution to these people in this context?"

"How am I protecting my sense of belonging no matter what happens?"

"Am I creating a safe place for others to feel belonging?"

In order to belong and build belonging, you must be clear in your identity, rooted in virtues, and be able to trust and be trustworthy. For Sonja and Hilary, a sense of belonging requires two decisions. The first is to identify and decide to whom you feel a sense of belonging. These people continually lift you up and provide space where you can express vulnerability and celebrate your virtues. The second is to decide what your contribution will be to your people, which are the actions you take that maintain the high trust relationships where you are supporting and lifting others in how they show up.

Who in your life needs to feel a sense of belonging? Maybe that person is you. The third mantra is waiting for you to complete below. Think carefully, and then repeat this mantra as an affirmation of your commitment to belonging.

Decide. Say it. Repeat it. Live it.

The DH Effect Belonging Mantra:
I commit to creating a safe, loving space for _____.

You Are the DH Effect

Creating positive change in the world starts with you—you showing up in all your brilliance. Stepping into your brilliant purpose starts with a decision. Decide what you will bring to this world and live it. Live it so confidently that you attract others, in all their light, to you. Build high trust relationships so that you can grow and become the best version of yourself. Finally, create a sense of belonging so that you always support and feel supported in your decided heart. Truly, stepping into your brilliant purpose is just a decision away, and to help you create your DH Effect, remember to visit these mantras often:

The DH Effect Self-Discovery Mantra:
I show up with _____.

The DH Effect Trust-Building Mantra:
As I trust myself, I extend healthy trust to others.

The DH Effect Belonging Mantra:
I commit to creating a safe, loving space for _____.

We look forward to seeing you step into your brilliant purpose one mantra, one step at a time.

Sonja Montiel and Hilary Bilbrey

Sonja Montiel and Hilary Bilbrey found trust and belonging in one another just before the pandemic and decided to come together to create a space where they could model authentic conversations and self-discovery. They did so in the form of a YouTube channel and podcast called "The DH Effect—The Decided Heart Effect." Their mission has now evolved, guiding individuals, schools, and organizations to personal accountability, high-trust relationships, and belonging.

Sonja and Hilary come with over forty years of experience in college admissions, life coaching, education, parenting, marriage, and friendship. As one of their guests so eloquently put it, "Sonja and Hilary are on a mission to love, inspire, and uplift this world," one decided heart at a time.

Email: thedheffect@gmail.com
Website: https://www.thedheffect.com
Facebook: https://www.facebook.com/DecidedHeartEffect
LinkedIn: https://www.linkedin.com/company/the-dh-effect
Twitter: https://twitter.com/dh_effect
YouTube:
https://www.youtube.com/channel/UCLznsYmBlX_lkM1YZ1t1G7g
Instagram: https://www.instagram.com/decided_heart_effect

DECLUTTER TO STEP INTO YOUR PURPOSE
BY ALISON KERO

"Geez, is there anything you do like about me?" I can't entirely fault this person for voicing what they probably felt were myriad concerns about me and my life, but after two days of him pointing out all my perceived faults, I had to ask. In response, I received a mere five seconds' worth of praise. At that moment, I felt like I was worthless in the eyes of one of the most important people in my life.

It didn't help that at the same time, a client, someone who had spent her career helping other women, was also seemingly unhappy with everything I did. Except in her case, she kept threatening to fire me and sabotaging my efforts while simultaneously praising me and offering me a full-time position with her.

Unsurprisingly, during all this insanity, I got sick.

I didn't just get sick. I got really, really sick. It was the flu, I think, but I couldn't get in to see my doctor, despite numerous calls. I finally got them to send in a prescription, but by then, I think it was too late to do me any good.

I had a fever of 102.3 that rose in an hour to 103.2. I was so nauseated that I could barely eat and lost twenty-five pounds without trying. That extreme nausea would last for another three to four years.

While the fever finally abated, it took three weeks before I could finally get out of bed. It took another six years before I finally found the help and support I needed to get and stay well. And that was just the tip of the iceberg in terms of what was to come.

But it was also during this time of chaos, uncertainty, isolation, fear, desperation, loneliness, and exhaustion that I found the system that would help me create the life I always wanted.

Clutter

No matter what form clutter takes, it feels chaotic, overwhelming, and exhausting. This is why it's not surprising that physical clutter is linked to anxiety and depression. I was so tired from the years of clutter I'd been collecting that I literally felt as though I was exhausted down to the bottom of my soul.

It's incredibly hard to care about anything when you're that tired. Making it even more challenging was that most of my clutter wasn't physical stuff like too much clothing or too many books. I'm a professional organizer, after all. I didn't have a ton of stuff in my home. What I had was a ton of stuff in my head that had been collecting for decades, and since I had ignored it for so long, it had begun manifesting as a physical illness.

Most of my clients struggle because their clutter is so overwhelming, they don't know where to begin. With all my emotional and physical health clutter, I felt at a loss of where to begin. But with any kind of clutter, you begin by picking one category and tackling one thing at a time. It's the only way that I have found is truly effective.

Goals

Some people find it hard to set goals, much less reach them. I'm one of them. I've got failing down to a science; what I've struggled with is finding and keeping success. I thought I knew what I wanted, but for a very long time, it seemed like the harder I tried, the worse things got. If I got one step forward, I'd end up knocked back several steps.

This was particularly frustrating when I was trying everything within my power to try to make lasting changes, especially in regard to my health.

I now understand that the way to create and realize a goal is to focus on the emotion. That's what we all want, after all. The goal isn't about having a well-organized closet. What we really want is a closet filled with items we like, fit us well, and want to wear. Our well-organized closets should make us feel happy and like we can conquer anything, no matter what we're wearing.

Boundaries

I found that the best system for achieving the goals/feelings I wanted to experience was to first identify the emotions I knew I no longer wanted to feel. But without boundaries, it's really easy for that same old clutter to sneak back in and thwart my attempts at lasting change.

In other words, if I want to feel loved and safe, keeping friends around who expect me to solve their problems while being unavailable when I need them isn't going to work any longer. That began to feel like I was letting my friends dump their garbage in my home every time I spoke with them.

Instead, I had to create healthy boundaries like speaking up and telling people I don't like being spoken to in harsh, rude, or unkind ways. It meant sticking to my boundaries when others (or myself) tried to break through them. And it sometimes means letting go of people or situations when my boundaries aren't respected.

Is it easy? No. Does it work? Yes.

Awareness and Intuition

I find I can't solve a problem until I'm aware there is one. That's not always easy to identify, especially when it's your own emotional clutter. It's sort of like having a favorite shirt. You wear it because it makes you feel great. The problems start when I fail to notice that my favorite shirt is getting stained and worn.

Old behaviors and systems are like that shirt. Sometimes it's hard to realize or even admit that something that once felt good no longer is.

I chose to declutter my tangible stuff first because I knew I had to get back in touch with my feelings in a safe way. It's easier to toss out an old sweater I haven't worn in three years than it is to walk away from old habits or toxic relationships. Once I get rid of the sweater, it's gone forever. It can't knock on my door or text me out of the blue just as I'm moving on with my life.

While I had plenty of space for my belongings, there were plenty of items I no longer needed, used, or even liked. I justified keeping things because I had the space. And at the time, having empty space felt scary to me. Now I realize that more space was exactly what I needed in my life.

I forced myself to go through literally everything I owned, one category at a time. I started with my wardrobe because I believe that it's the easiest but most profound decluttering process. It's easier because there's usually the least amount of emotional attachment associated with clothes. And it's profound because once I narrowed my choices of what to wear down to items that fit me well and looked good on me, it changed how I looked and felt about myself.

I then went through everything ending with the hardest, most emotional stuff, which was my photographs.

Each time, I first had to become aware of what I owned. I needed to pull everything out so that I could see what I had and what I was surrounding myself with. Awareness allowed me to use actual facts to help me make smarter decisions about what I really needed and wanted in my life.

Intuition

Decluttering gave me space to actually think and hear myself for once. I was able to finally listen to my intuition to find out what I wanted and needed in my life. And it helped me make some tough decisions about who and what I wanted in my life.

I realized that without the clutter, I felt exhausted spending time with certain people rather than energized. I felt as though I was doing everything and had surrounded myself with people who were willing to take what I gave them but were rarely willing to give back. This included friends, clients, medical professionals, and even strangers.

My intuition was telling me that I had been giving for a long time but had stopped being able to receive much, if at all. And that lack of receiving came in a wide variety of forms from lack of medical health, a safe space to live, feeling loved, and having financial security.

Listening to my intuition helped me realize that I needed to make the space and put boundaries in place so I could finally start surrounding myself with an actual support system. My intuition also told me exactly who I could and should trust and who would make my life more difficult.

Creating a new system helped me make my life easier, so I could utilize what little energy I had to be as productive as possible.

Decision-making

The way I look at life, you either have stuff in yours that helps you achieve your goals, or you have stuff that prohibits you from ever getting anything you want. Some might think that being thin or rich are their real goals, but what I think it all boils down to is most of us just want to feel healthy, happy, and safe.

I know I do. And when I fully understood what my true goals were, it got a lot easier to figure out where I needed to put up boundaries. I finally felt I knew what I wanted, and I could then set up healthy boundaries to help me make smart decisions.

This system also helped me finally hear myself. And when I realized that when I listened and followed through with what my intuition was telling me, things were turning out okay. Even pretty well in some circumstances. And I wasn't getting knocked back several steps anymore. I also found it was easier to think clearly and not make choices based on other people's opinions on what they thought I "should" do.

Do I still ignore the warning signals?

Sometimes. I recently hired someone who gave me immediate signals he wasn't right for the job. But I ignored my gut because I was really tired. After hiring him, I did not stick to my boundaries and chose not to speak up when the red flags started appearing. Unsurprisingly, the clutter began building up until we reached an impasse.

It cost me time and money. But what it didn't cost me was more clutter because I put my boundaries back in place as soon as I realized I was off-track. I still stray from my system now and then. It's sometimes easier to stick with the old ways, especially when I feel tired.

But I also am a lot more sensitive to the clutter now. I've had tons of practice because I've decluttered a lot of stuff. I know what it looks and feels like because of all that practice. I'm also a lot less tolerant of it, which means even when I don't set up the right boundaries straight away, it's still easier to deal with before it becomes an unmanageable nightmare.

I also try not to add more emotional and spiritual clutter to my life by beating myself up when I don't make smart decisions. And I know that my life works better when I have tools set in place to help me figure out what I want and how to eliminate all the potential roadblocks.

Change is scary, even when it's a change I actually want. But I also know this system allows me to grow and change as I need to. It lets me forge my own path and puts me in control of my life.

We cannot allow new things in when there is too much clutter. We must make space for the new to come in. Creating a system that allows us to be in control of when and how we make space for new things helps us walk forward into our purposes filled with anticipation and excitement rather than fear.

Tips to Declutter and Make Room for Your Purpose:

1. **Clutter check-in**: What is adding clutter to your life?
2. **Emotions**: Bring emotions into helping you drive your goals.
3. **Boundaries**: Establish clear boundaries and honor them.
4. **Awareness and Intuition**: Pay attention to your surroundings and emotions.
5. **Decision-making**: Use the above tools to help you make smart decisions for yourself.

Alison Kero

Alison Kero is a professional organizer with over fifteen years of experience, as well as the owner of Alison Kero Organizing. She began her career in NYC in 2004 but has since worked with clients throughout the United States.

Since she started her career, Alison has written a book, sat on two boards, been a guest on various podcasts, and was a featured writer discussing organizational tips for the now-defunct Hearst-owned publication, Manilla.com.

In 2014, Alison became extremely ill with what she later discovered was Lyme disease. For nearly six years, Alison struggled to get back on her feet. Thankfully, after she began to use her skills as an organizer, Alison was able to create a system to help her regain her health, her career, and her life.

Besides teaching people how to get and stay organized, Alison is passionate about mental health and helping the environment. She believes that learning organizing skills can help people be happier and keep the planet healthier.

Alison currently lives in Myrtle Beach, South Carolina.

Email: alison@alisonkero.com
Phone: 646-831-9625
Website: https://www.alisonkero.com
LinkedIn: https://linkedin.com/in/alisonkero
YouTube: https://www.youtube.com/c/alisonkero
Instagram: https://www.instagram.com/keroalison

CLOSING THOUGHTS

REBECCA HALL GRUYTER, COMPILER AND MAUREEN RYAN BLAKE, COMPILER

We hope you have been touched by these powerful chapters that have encouraged, equipped, and empowered you to step into your brilliant purpose! We can't wait to see you, hear from you, and celebrate you as you share your gift of you with the world! May you always choose to *live on purpose and with great purpose.*

Anthologies Compiled by Rebecca Hall Gruyter:

<u>SHINE Series</u> (compiled and led by Rebecca Hall Gruyter)
    Come out of Hiding and SHINE! (Book 1)
    Bloom Where You Are Planted and SHINE! (Book 2)
    Step Forward and SHINE! (Book 3)

<u>Step Into Series</u> (compiled and led by Rebecca Hall Gruyter)
    Step into Your Brilliance! (Book 1)
    Step into Your Brilliant Purpose! (Book 2)

<u>Experts and Influencers Series</u> (compiled and led by Rebecca Hall Gruyter)
    Experts and Influencers Series: Leadership (Book 1)
    Experts and Influencers Series: Women's Empowerment (Book 2)
    Experts and Influencers Series: Step Forward with Purpose (Book 3)

The Grandmother Legacies (anthology compiled by Rebecca Hall Gruyter)

The Animal Legacies (anthology compiled by Rebecca Hall Gruyter)

Bloom & SHINE! (365 daily inspiration anthology compiled by Rebecca Hall Gruyter)

Empowering YOU, Transforming Lives (365 daily inspiration anthology compiled by Rebecca Hall Gruyter)

Books Featuring a Chapter by Rebecca Hall Gruyter:

The 40/40 Rules, anthology compiled by Holly Porter

Becoming Outrageously Successful, anthology compiled by Dr. Anita Jackson

Bright Spots, anthology compiled by Davis Creative

Catch Your Star, anthology published by THRIVE Publishing

Discover Your Destiny, anthology compiled by Denise Joy Thompson

Engaging Experts, anthology compiled by Davis Creative

I Am Beautiful, anthology compiled by Teresa Hawley-Howard

Movers & Shakers 2020, anthology compiled by Teresa Hawley-Howard

The Power of Our Voices, Sharing Our Story, anthology compiled by Teresa Hawley-Howard

Real Estate Investing for Women, anthology compiled by Moneeka Sawyer

Succeeding Against All Odds, anthology compiled by Sandra Yancey

Success Secrets for Today's Feminine Entrepreneurs, anthology compiled by Dr. Anita Jackson

Unstoppable Woman of Purpose, anthology and workbook, compiled by Nella Chikwe

Women on a Mission, anthology compiled by Teresa Hawley-Howard

Women of Courage, Women of Destiny, anthology compiled by Dr. Anita Jackson

Women Warriors Who Make It Rock, anthology compiled by Nichole Peters

You Are Whole, Perfect, and Complete – Just as You Are, compiled by Carol Plummer and Susan Driscoll

Books Featuring a Chapter by Maureen Ryan Blake:

Bloom & SHINE! Daily inspiration anthology compiled by Rebecca Hall Gruyter

Experts and Influencers Series: Step Forward with Purpose, anthology compiled by Rebecca Hall Gruyter

Journals by Rebecca Hall Gruyter:

The Animal Legacies Journal

The Experts and Influencers Leadership Journal

The Experts and Influencers Move Forward with Purpose Journal

Women's Empowerment Journal

Step into Your Brilliance Journal

Step into Your Brilliant Purpose Journal

Dear Powerful Reader,

Thank you for reading our anthology. We hope it has encouraged and empowered you and uplifted you in the area of leadership. Listed below, please find out a little bit more about each of the compilers that have come together to create this powerful book for you.

RHG Media Productions and Your Purpose Driven Practice™

I wanted to share a little bit more about our organizations, Your Purpose Driven Practice™, RHG TV Network™, RHG Publishing™, and RHG Media Productions™. We are passionate about helping others live on purpose and with purpose in their lives and business. I hope this book has supported and inspired you to choose to live on purpose and with great purpose in your leadership!

If you want to reach more people and be part of inspiring and supporting others with your message, your gifts, and the work that you bring to the world, then I want to share some opportunities for you to consider.

Each year we compile and produce anthology book projects, support authors in publishing their own powerful books as bestsellers, produce and publish an international magazine, launch TV shows, facilitate women's empowerment conferences, get quoted in major media, launch radio and podcast shows, and help experts and speakers step into a place of powerful influence to make a global difference. We provide programs and strategies to help you reach more people and facilitate the Speaker Talent Search (which helps speakers, experts, and influencers connect with more speaking opportunities). We would love to support you in reaching more people. Please take a moment to learn a little bit more about us at the sites listed below, and then reach out to us for a conversation. **We would love to help you be seen, heard, and SHINE!**

You can learn more about each of these things on our main website: www.YourPurposeDrivenPractice.com

Enjoy our powerful **TV and podcast shows**: www.RHGTVNetwork.com

Learn more about the **Speaker Talent Search™**:

www.SpeakerTalentSearch.com

Learn more about our **writing opportunities**: http://yourpurposedrivenpractice.com/writing-opportunities/

If you would like to connect with me personally to explore some of our opportunities in upcoming book projects, podcast/radio shows, and/or TV, then here is the link to schedule a time to speak with me directly: www.MeetWithRebecca.com, or you can email me at: Rebecca@YourPuposeDrivenPractice.com.

May you always choose to be seen, heard, and SHINE!

Warmly,

Rebecca Hall Gruyter

Other book projects I participated in:

Bloom and SHINE! Author (365 daily inspiration anthology compiled by Rebecca Hall Gruyter)

The Power of the Tribe Network

I would love to connect and support you in standing in your brilliant purpose. The Power of the Tribe Network is all about women coming together in unity. I know this anthology has inspired you, and I look forward to seeing you claiming your voice and standing in your power.

> *"When a woman loses her tribe, she loses her shine.*
> *But when women come together, we shine brighter."*
> —Maureen Ryan Blake

Here are some ways we support our clients to shine. We work with our clients to elevate and increase their visibility.

Learn more about us: https://thepowerofthetribe.com

I would love to connect with you.

Maureen Ryan Blake

www.ingramcontent.com/pod-product-compliance
Lightning Source LLC
Chambersburg PA
CBHW070916080526
44589CB00013B/1312